More Praise

DEM
CAM

"[A] darkly brilliant book . . . Remarkable . . . Startling, precise prose."
—Jeff Sharlet, *Bookforum*

"Visceral, seductive . . . It's hard to pull away. . . . Percy's narrative artfully upsets a common misperception: that all veterans' experiences of war are alike."
—*New York Times Book Review*

"Thrilling . . . Percy is onto something essential here: understanding PTSD is one key to understanding our present cultural moment. . . . Arrives at an unlikely awareness of our shared humanity . . ."
—*The Daily Beast*

"This is the book I've been waiting for. Lyrical, haunting, surreal, as fiercely brave as it is fearsome, Jen Percy's *Demon Camp* is both damning and redemptive, a shot straight to the hellish heart of war."
—Kim Barnes, author of *In the Kingdom of Men*

"If you want to understand America now, read Jen Percy's *Demon Camp*. An electric, unflinchingly brave, and entirely necessary debut."
—Alexander Chee, author of *Edinburgh*

"Haunting . . . Exposes the raw reality of pain and loss. Many of us have read and heard about the post-traumatic stress disorder . . . Percy has lifted the veil for us."
—*Pittsburgh Post-Gazette*

"Percy has taken a sensationalistic, tabloid-worthy subject and explored it in a remarkably clear-eyed and empathetic fashion, without a trace of condescension. *Demon Camp* is not only luminously written and exhaustively researched; it's an important account of post-traumatic stress disorder in modern warfare."
—Teddy Wayne, author of *The Love Song of Jonny Valentine*

"The writing is beautiful. . . . Percy has a photographer's eye. . . . She deftly makes this story part of a bigger picture—for her, what happened to Caleb Daniels is a key to understanding the way America deals with war and its aftermath."

—*The Portland Oregonian*

"Beneath the taut, wry surface of Jen Percy's *Demon Camp* is a deeply felt investigation that is marvelously disturbing—a pitch-perfect blend of reportage, meditation, and outright fantasy that beautifully captures the wounds of mind and heart in ruins."

—John D'Agata, author of *The Lifespan of a Fact*

"Jen Percy delves deep into the life of an army vet suffering from post-traumatic stress to understand the effect of war on returning soldiers. . . . You can't walk away from Percy's strong debut without feeling like you've spent a frightening moment inside the heads of soldiers who come home from war with nothing but demons, no place to go and no easy role to play."

—*Shelf Awareness* (starred review)

"*Demon Camp* is the most urgent, most harrowing book to yet emerge from our wars in Iraq and Afghanistan. Percy is a brave and relentlessly powerful witness, again and again confronting us with the monsters of our own making. Written with haunting austerity, this exceptionally important book must be read not only by every voter but by every one of us yearning to be more humane."

—Claire Vaye Watkins, author of *Battleborn*

"Percy's book gets so close to its subject's consciousness that it stops being about any social issue, the way *The Executioner's Song* isn't really 'about' the psychology of killers. It's the most unusual and beautiful portrait of trauma to come out of the last thirteen years."

—Jesse Barron, *The New Inquiry*

"[*Demon Camp*] shines a bright light on America's wounded psyche. . . . Percy's beautiful, lucid writing takes the reader into the lives of soldiers wrestling with faith in this often harrowing book on the personal, cultural, and political costs of war."

—*Los Angeles Times*

"A triumph of reporting, storytelling, and sympathy. Percy writes as if possessed, not by her own demons but by the war-torn lives she documents. Like some pilgrim in a latter-day *Inferno*, with machine gunner Sergeant Caleb Daniels for her Virgil, she has descended into an all-American hell, eyes open, notebook in hand, and returned with this haunted and haunting fever-dream of a book."

—Donovan Hohn, author of *Moby-Duck*

"*Demon Camp* is the amazing story of one man's journey to war and back. It's a tale so extraordinary that at times it seems conjured from a dream; as it unfolds it's not just Caleb Daniels that comes into focus, but America, too. Jen Percy has orchestrated a great narrative about redemption, loss, and hope."

—Dexter Filkins, Pulitzer Prize–winning author of *The Forever War*

"Tropes surrounding veterans in the public discourse mask the reality of warfare, but Percy peels back the gauze, revealing deeply wounded individuals. . . . Her sharp, unadorned writing captures the rawness of the congregants' lives, the permeability of the borderline between reality and imagination."

—*Publishers Weekly*

"This wild journey alongside madness leads Percy to the place where myth is conceived and destroyed, our wars overseas brought home as nightmares. You will begin to wonder how much pain is dreamed and if fantasy might be the way to cure it. A unique, fascinating, and always surprising book."

—Benjamin Busch, author of *Dust to Dust*

"[A] talented young writer . . . Chilling and raw."

—*Winnipeg Free Press*

"With exquisite patience, a wide-open mind, and a willingness that trembles on vulnerability to immerse herself in her subject, Jen Percy recounts the terrible, ongoing struggles of soldiers whom the war has followed home. Writing in lucid, beautiful sentences, Percy exposes the great psychic cost of the Bush-era wars as paid by these young men and gives us to understand that their demons are America's demons, their stories, America's stories."

—Michelle Huneven, author of *Jamesland* and *Blame*

"A chilling work of narrative nonfiction."

—*O, The Oprah Magazine*

"*Demon Camp* is for fans of Michael Herr's *Dispatches* or Hunter Thompson's own dark journeys through America; indeed, it's hard to describe *Demon Camp* as anything but a tour de force literary experience: exquisitely written, psychologically deft and nimble, and shocking. Jen Percy writes a book that is at once so singular that it speaks to despair and joy yawing over our collective horizon. Here is a new, utterly surprising world we can scarcely imagine being in, except in Percy's hands."

—Doug Stanton, *New York Times*–bestselling author of *Horse Soldiers*

"A powerful debut . . . A haunting portrait of PTSD and the effects of war on the psyches of the soldiers who fight . . ."

—*Esquire*

"Ambitious . . . What Daniels, and Percy as his medium, has provided is a meditation on trauma, a haunted interior made external: an exorcism provided by the text. It is a rough-and-tumble first book for Percy and a remarkable one."

—*Tottenville Review*

"Percy has walked far out into the Twilight Zone and leads us into realms of horror and dread, mystery and high weirdness. I have never read anything quite like it."

—Luis Alberto Urrea, author of *The Devil's Highway*

DEMON CAMP

The Strange and Terrible Saga
of a Soldier's Return from War

JEN PERCY

SCRIBNER

New York London Toronto Sydney New Delhi

SCRIBNER
A Division of Simon & Schuster, Inc.
1230 Avenue of the Americas
New York, NY 10020

First Scribner trade paperback edition February 2015

SCRIBNER and design are registered trademarks of The Gale Group, Inc.,
used under license by Simon & Schuster, Inc., the publisher of this work.

For information about special discounts for bulk purchases,
please contact Simon & Schuster Special Sales at 1-866-506-1949
or business@simonandschuster.com.

The Simon & Schuster Speakers Bureau can bring authors to your live event.
For more information or to book an event contact the Simon & Schuster Speakers Bureau
at 1-866-248-3049 or visit our website at www.simonspeakers.com.

Manufactured in the United States of America

1 3 5 7 9 10 8 6 4 2

Library of Congress Control Number: 2014395398

ISBN 978-1-4516-6198-9
ISBN 978-1-4516-6206-1 (pbk)
ISBN 978-1-4516-6208-5 (ebook)

Certain names and identifying characteristics have been changed.
Originally published with the subtitle *A Soldier's Exorcism*.

To understand original sin is to understand Adam, which is to understand that one is an individual and one is also part of the whole race.

—KIERKEGAARD, *The Concept of Dread*

Dreams remained. For years afterwards in nightmares stark as archive footage, I was what I had been.

—JAMES SALTER, *Burning the Days*

CONTENTS

DEMON
CAMP

A BRIEF HISTORY
OF THE DISORDERLY
CONDUCT OF THE HEART

Sergeant Caleb Daniels wanted to save all the veterans from killing themselves. A machine gunner three years out of the 160th Special Operations Regiment, 3rd Battalion, he'd tried to kill himself, four or five times, but he was interrupted each time—once by his dead buddy Kip Jacoby; once by his girlfriend Krissy, whom he met at a strip club; once on a lake by his house in his canoe when the rain stopped and he saw the moon; and once when the demon called the Black Thing came into his bedroom in Savannah and said, "I will kill you if you proceed," and Caleb said, "No you won't, asshole, because I'm going to do it myself."

At first Caleb thought he was crazy because he saw dead people, but then his roommate's new stepdad, Wombly, a member of the Lakota tribe, saw a dead kid soldier with Alice in Wonderland tattoos following Caleb around the house. It was Kip Jacoby, whom Caleb had last seen on the tarmac at Bagram Air Force Base, slipping inside the belly of an MH-47 Chinook nicknamed *Evil Empire*—tail #146—the same Chinook that would explode in a remote region of the Hindu Kush forty-five minutes later, killing all sixteen men aboard, including eight members of his unit.

Wombly took Caleb to a sweat lodge down the street to teach him how to become a medicine man, worship their buffalo god, and talk to the dead soldiers who had followed him home. Caleb saw bodies appearing and disappearing in the smoke, old Indian warriors, crows and bats and wolves. At first Caleb thought he'd gained power sufficient to make the Black Thing go away, but the Black Thing didn't go away.

Caleb met another veteran who also saw the Black Thing and knew how to fight it. So the veteran and Caleb drove to demon camp in Portal, Georgia, where the layer between heaven and earth is very thin, and Caleb sat down in a chair in a trailer and got an exorcism from a group of strangers, and he found his ruling demon wasn't PTSD, like the doctors said, it was a six-foot, five-inch buffalo with horns—a manifestation of the war demon known as Destroyer. That's when he realized it wasn't for no reason he didn't die on that Chinook, #146, the *Evil Empire*. The mission, he decided, was in America now. He knew the only way to save the vets from killing themselves was to kill the Black Thing first. He started a company, a factory in the woods that would hire a veterans-only workforce to rebuild old military vehicles—machines that would give life instead of destroying it. Then he'd use the profits from this company to counsel soldiers into not killing themselves. Some would recover with counseling, but some would not. Then he'd send these soldiers to demon camp for deliverance from the Destroyer. A modern-day exorcism of the trauma of war.

When I first met Caleb, one morning in June 2008, in an isolated parking lot beside the Allatoona Reservoir in the woods near Kennesaw, Georgia, he told me he wanted to talk about how the war had followed him home. But by lunchtime, over cheese enchiladas at the Mi Casa Mexican Restaurant, in a strip mall ten miles from the site where in 1864, 2,321 soldiers died in a single day at the Battle of Kennesaw Mountain, he told me instead about the thing that followed him home from the war, the thing in the burning peach trees, the thing in the sandstorms and the dried riverbeds, the thing in the camel spiders that walked in the shadows of soldiers. It followed him across the Atlantic and sat beside him in the jet where he carried Kip Jacoby's body home. It followed him to Florida where Kip's father wanted an open casket and Caleb had to bring him to the morgue to convince him otherwise. It followed him back to Georgia and to Missouri, where he was born. Somewhere between Mi Casa and Portal, because Caleb said these things could transfer, and because these things are not limited to war, I started to wonder if it was following me.

PART I

WAR DREAMS

The way he remembered it, the war was going to save him. There was no war yet, but there was the dream of it anyway. It was going to save him from the fields of Centralia, Missouri, a town where most kids wanted saving, knowing that beyond Centralia was a world as wide and unfilled as the wheat that spread like rolled carpet from their porches. In Centralia night came without a neighbor's lit window and morning came without the sounds of turning tires or the echoes of children. The nearest city was twenty miles away and the wind—loud and fierce and ceaseless—made the wheat bend like men in prayer. It tore at the grain, lifting pieces into the air so that at times the fields looked like great swaths of insects.

The war was going to save him from the poverty of his mother's wages at the Eastern Airways ticket counter. Some days she put Caleb on board and the pilots let him fly jump seat, and the landscape of his youth grew small and the horizon breathed opportunity. Nights, he dreamed of flight. Since the second grade, he wanted to be a military pilot. Somehow or another he knew he would go to war because the war was going to save him from his father, who divorced his mother when he was thirteen, leaving the house filled with traces of parents no longer in love, the halls still echoing with his mother's screams. There were the days his father screamed at him, too, for not hitting a home run at the Little League game. He said the military wouldn't even take Caleb. It was the war that was going to save him from the poor grades, the whiskey smells, the unexcused absences, the hallway fights, and the plum-sized bleeding eyeball his mother must have cooled gently with a frozen bag of peas. He needed saving from the days spent riding bareback in the rodeo, the thrill he felt in the ring's quiet center, and the women who watched, wearing sequins and drinking cold Cherry Coke.

The war was going to save him from the agony of love: a girl named Allyson. The way it goes in Centralia is that you date and then you get married, and because Allyson always knew Caleb would get out, they started dating in the summer of 1997, when Caleb was sixteen, and on into harvest season, air thick with grain smells, doing the usual things: rubbing each other in the backs of cold theaters, tonguing salt-plastered lips, or just sitting in fields back to back with the wheat reigning all around them. On weekends he worked her father's farm, rolling stiff veins of irrigation pipe, bringing water to places where there was none. Her father rarely got off the couch. One day he seemed to give up on life. That's when Caleb made promises to Allyson, said he'd get her out of Centralia. One day they met on the back of a tractor in a bean field; Allyson told Caleb that while he'd been gone she'd started seeing a classmate named Cole Boy. So when he left for the war, he left her too.

Middle of sophomore year, sixteen years old, and he dropped out of Centralia High School. He'd already received emancipation from his parents. The GED wasn't hard. He looked for work. The only place hiring was in the nearby city of Columbia, at the college, the hospital, and the AB Chance Company, where men worked with gloved hands inside a metal building for long hours forming ship anchors from soft iron, and at a company that had no name, just a man, Scott, who fixed steel buildings abandoned across the flat wilderness of Missouri, Kansas, and Illinois. He paid eighteen dollars an hour and Caleb waited for him in a parking lot at Home Depot while clouds of gnats rose from the plots of switchgrass that broke the pavement.

The men he joined were not good men. They were coke addicts and meth addicts and they ate steak for breakfast, working eighteen-hour shifts, seven days a week. Every other week they had Sunday off. At night all the men shared a hotel room, three men to a bed, five to a floor.

Caleb worked through harvest season into winter. From the road, the buildings looked like deep red slashes in the sky. They leaned. He liked climbing to the top of the buildings, where the voices below seemed too weak to rise, and everywhere there was the mingling of heat and cold—the backs of tractors collecting snowfall, livestock pooling amid rising steam.

December came, and the farmers retreated to their homes and the livestock walked defeated to their barns to feed on old grain.

The manner of the work was most likely illegal. They'd make bets: rebuild from the ground up in ten days, all or nothing. The guys were always yelling at each other. Guys falling off the tops of buildings because they were tiptoeing along inch-wide steel beams with nothing to tie on to. They used an old forklift with a broken emergency brake to hoist themselves forty feet in the air. One of the guys got the idea to put an old piece of fence on the fork, flat like a platform, and they huddled atop it like birds to work.

One day Caleb was up on the forklift, welding a roof ledge, when the driver went into a cocaine rage and abandoned the vehicle. It rolled backward. Caleb jumped at the last minute, grabbed onto the roof ledge. Behind him, the forklift slammed into an eighteen-wheeler box truck and erupted into flames. The workers gathered around the fire, forgetting Caleb, who dangled by his fingertips until blisters grew soft between the metal and his skin. The screws rattled beneath his grip. Twenty minutes passed before they noticed. They picked him up off the roof with another forklift and lowered him to the ground. Caleb asked for a check and told them he was on his way to something else.

Snow fell, covered the highway. He passed the brokenness of grain silos, billboards for adult stores, McDonald's signs rising over the fields like the sun itself.

Ten miles out, somewhere near Right City, Missouri, the road going straight through farm country, a blizzard began, and up ahead, on the icy roads, two cars collided. Caleb came to a halt. A man in a white Ford Taurus had hit another car, and the whole front of his truck was mangled.

One driver dead. The other in bad shape. An old man with blood and glass all over his face. The door was crushed-in, so Caleb couldn't pull it open to remove him. But because the dome light was sparking and there was fuel everywhere, Caleb grabbed the old man and tried to drag him through the window. His ribs were so badly broken that they crumbled and snapped against Caleb's hand like a tangle of rotten branches. He was shivering, bleeding in deep pools. At that moment another car pulled up and a man in an army uniform got out. Together they yanked off the driver's side door and pulled the old man from the vehicle. A state trooper arrived and though Caleb asked for help, he wouldn't give it. Caleb, infuriated, snatched the hat from the trooper's head and put it on the old man. They stood over him. He handed Caleb a photograph. Tell my wife I love her, the old man said. Then he died.

The EMTs had to push Caleb off the body. The old man disappeared with the ambulance lights, leaving Caleb kneeling on the road in snow smeared bright as cherries.

He turned around and looked at the soldier.

"I need to get out of here," he said. "Is there anything you can do for me?"

The soldier nodded. He was a recruiter for the U.S. Army and he took Caleb to a diner down the highway. They drank coffee. Hours later, they drove to the recruitment office.

Caleb went home. He didn't tell his mother about his day. He didn't call Allyson. Instead he ate a quiet dinner, and he went to bed, and in the middle of the night he filled his backpack with a toothbrush and a change of clothes and he snuck out his bedroom window into the Missouri cold. He drove straight through Illinois, Kentucky, Tennessee, and Georgia and all the way to Fort Jackson, South Carolina, where a sign hanging on the wall read: VICTORY STARTS HERE.

One of thousands and nervous as a bird. They ate shoulder to shoulder. There were fences between him and the world now, long roads, wires, and phone calls and messages still to be read. What he did mattered now. It mattered to the group. Drill Sergeant Barganier—a real mean guy, six-foot-five, skinny limbs—scrambled his brain into something new. The day Caleb was promoted to platoon leader over his class, he felt the addiction of hard work. A thing once unrewarded, now turned into gifts.

When Caleb finally told his mother what he'd done, the phone was pressed to his ear, greased with the hands of other men. He waited for her to be proud, but she only begged Caleb to call Allyson because Allyson had been calling every night, sometimes at three or four in the morning, wondering where he'd gone. "She's driving me crazy trying to find out where you've been." Caleb's mother hated Allyson. Allyson accused her of lying about not knowing the whos and whats of her son.

In time, he did call Allyson and she said she wanted to be with him, and because he was lonely and away from home, he said he wanted to be with her too. Every day Caleb snuck her these little one-minute phone calls and they'd talk, exchanging apologies and promises.

Caleb's mother worried he wasn't going to graduate basic training. Caleb's father straight out said he'd fail. The words crowded him. Caleb considered quitting because he didn't want to lose Allyson. Away from her now, he believed in her. He went to Sergeant Barganier and told him he was having some problems at home. "I don't think I am cracked up to this."

Barganier said the solution was real easy. He said, "I'm going to make the decision for you. I'm not filing the paperwork. You're not going home, and if you try to go home then I'm going to tie you up here so long that you can't leave."

His mother and brother showed up to the graduation. Allyson didn't. He didn't remember her even being there. The army shipped him to advanced training in Fort Eustis, Virginia, outside the small fishing town of Newport News, where he trained as a helicopter mechanic, fixing Black Hawks and Chinooks.

At Eustis, Caleb had enough freedom to remember what freedom was like, but he was caged up and he couldn't enjoy anything. He wasn't allowed to have a car. Mostly he missed Allyson and his little brother, John. The other soldiers talked about sex and the ways of women and he didn't know much. He felt himself retreating in these moments. Disappearing. He was younger than the other guys. If his grades were 80 percent or better, he'd get a pass and he could leave for the weekend. He'd go to the bars with his buddies and they'd stay at hotels.

Caleb kept dating Allyson, but over time he sensed a drifting in her voice. She was still talking to Cole Boy. "You're gone too much," she said. So he called this other girl he knew from home named Gillian, who lived in Atlanta. "You know I've crushed on you since seventh grade," he told her. "I was just too worked up about skipping school and riding rodeo to give you the time of day." A Greyhound got him to Atlanta, and the two had plans to meet, but when he arrived his friend Smitty dragged him to a bar. Caleb stood her up.

A few days later, they met and drove to the beach on Tybee Island in Savannah and they stayed up all night talking and the talking was easy. They buried and unburied their feet. They sat on that beach and they must have talked for nine hours and it didn't feel like long. Never went further. She was a strong Catholic girl.

Twice a week Caleb and Gillian went to Taco Bell, and, once, he told her: "You've been nothing but sweet to me. I love you. But I'm not going to talk to you anymore until I get everything resolved at home. You get one phone call a day when I get all this baggage put behind me. Will you be there when I do all this?"

"I'll be here as long as I can," she said.

Allyson found out Caleb had those two weeks off. She started calling his father constantly. Caleb's father said he couldn't take it anymore. "Get her off my back," he said.

But it was too late, Allyson had left a message on Caleb's answering machine: I've used all my money. I bought a ticket to come to Hartsfield-Jackson Atlanta International Airport. One way. I don't have a way back home and I don't know my way around the airport, so you better be there. I'm just coming.

She arrived at Hartsfield-Jackson wearing a yellow dress and peach perfume. They rented a cabin for three days and Caleb noticed that things were different. It was pretty much the way it had been in Centralia. Sex, hot and heavy. That was it. There was no foundation to it at all. There was still that part of him that wanted to take care of her. He thought of her as helpless. She gave him that whole *I can't live without you* talk.

Back at Fort Eustis, after too many days spent lubricating drive systems, repairing cockpit gauges, checking tension on flight controls, Caleb decided he was lonely again. He was eighteen years old. He asked his buddy Smitty what to do: Should I go for the sexy one I don't like or the not so sexy one I do like?

Smitty said write a letter to both of them and tell them you're sorry and whichever one takes you back is the one it's supposed to be. Caleb wrote Allyson and Gillian the same letter and they both said *okay*. Smitty said the only way to do it now is to flip a coin. Good logic. So they flipped a coin. It landed on Allyson.

Allyson came down the day before he graduated from advanced training, a few months after the coin toss. It'd been a long time since he'd seen a girl. They got a hotel and toward the end of the weekend they were lying in bed. "Listen," Allyson said. "I went back to Cole Boy. We had sex a couple times but I realized he wasn't for me. You're the one I want."

The military guys at Eustis told Caleb it was a common thing and so he forgave her. At graduation she pinned on his airborne wings and smiled in pictures with just the two of them.

They drove back to Missouri and took a bit of leave and Allyson had this little red Plymouth piece of junk and he had a 1977 Ford pickup truck. He started working on it because he had one week to get it seaworthy enough to drive to Georgia. They rented a U-Haul trailer and put it behind the truck and they drove, Allyson in the Plymouth, and Caleb in the truck.

In a town called Dalton, in Georgia, his power steering went out. The only person he had to call with any money was his father. He said he was broke down with empty pockets. He had to report to the base by morning. His father gave him 146 bucks.

Allyson's mother found them an apartment in Statesboro, forty-five minutes away from Fort Stewart. It was a little one-bedroom apartment. It was a lot of really good sex and a lot of jealousy. Allyson didn't want Caleb in the army. She wanted to get married and have children and she wanted him to be home.

One time they were at a restaurant that sold thick hamburgers and she said, "There's a girl just walked in the door. Don't look at her." She must have compared every part of herself to this woman. Caleb wasn't cheating. She always thought he was cheating. Allyson stayed anyway and took classes at Georgia Southern. He'd try to talk to her about what was going on in the army. She said she hated the army.

Finally, unable to take it anymore, his long workdays, the uncertain future, she pinned him in the house. "I'm not letting you leave." Caleb punched a hole in the wall next to her head. Allyson stepped slowly to the side. An hour later, he came back. Nothing but a note saying she'd be gone for the night at a hotel. She'd taken his credit card. All night he was sorry and he painted these picture frames that she'd asked him to paint yellow.

Caleb and Allyson moved to Savannah next and he was stationed with Hunter Army Airfield base, working as a low-level army mechanic, a low-paid private, with the 159th Aviation Regiment.

Payroll messed up his check one month, and they had no money to pay the bills. Allyson wasn't working. Caleb called Smitty, and Smitty recommended they get married, and so they married because that added eight hundred dollars to his monthly paycheck, and because they could not leave each other, and because they were eighteen, and they hung crosses on their walls and this meant something. They married at the justice of the peace for thirty-five dollars and took a slow honeymoon at Red Lobster.

Caleb didn't know what marriage was supposed to be like except that you're gonna be miserable for the rest of your life and your wife is gonna bicker at you and life sucks. He thought, Well, this is what it's like to be married. Things shifted. Allyson had full rein to go crazy over anything. The jealousy got way worse. Any time the military would say, *be here at this time*, she'd say, *if you love me, you won't go*. It was hard enough to have to do it and then come home and hear her shit. He'd say, they'll throw me in jail if I don't go. Within six months they weren't even talking anymore.

One day, in the middle of all this, members of the 160th Aviation Regiment, a Special Forces helicopter transport crew known as the Night Stalkers, asked Caleb's unit for extra help doing phase work on their choppers. No one volunteered to go over. They'd heard rumors about those guys: that they were six-foot-tall snake-eaters, and throat-slitters, and that they did stuff you couldn't talk about, and you couldn't talk about them. Their motto was Death Waits in the Dark. Their creed, taken from the Book of Revelation: "And I looked, and behold a pale horse: and his name that sat on him was Death, and Hell followed with him. And power was given unto them over the fourth part of the earth, to kill with sword, and with hunger, and with death, and with the beasts of the earth."

Some said when Night Stalkers died in the field, they'd be decapitated, the hands removed and hidden in bags, separated from the body to prevent identification. Some said when a Night Stalker died in ways you couldn't tell his family about, they mutilated the body to launder it. Some said they'd run it over with a jeep, blow it up, douse it with oil, and set it on fire, invent a new truth.

The platoon leaders called on their four newest cherries, and Caleb, with only three months' experience, was sent over. He was surprised. They jogged in shorts instead of sweatpants and took on dangerous missions, mostly at night. They were a Special Ops regiment, flying Blackhawks, MH-47 Chinooks, Apache gunships, supporting dangerous combat missions of Special Forces recon teams. Caleb never wanted to go back to the 159th. He stayed a few weeks, fixing choppers, observing the men—their camaraderie and intensity.

He stopped by the sergeant major's open office hours and told him he wanted to become a Night Stalker. "What the fuck are you talking about, you pencil-dick pussy? You're nothing but a goddamn kid. Get the fuck out of my fucking office on the fucking double."

The sergeant major spit when he spoke. Caleb nodded at his words but came back every week for six weeks until he was escorted out by military personnel. Special Ops was divided between the guys who do stuff and the guys who don't. He learned that assessment is the way to get to do stuff. The guys who assess, they fly the helicopters, go into combat, shoot the bad guys. The guys who don't, they sit at a desk. Finally the sergeant major said, "You're not going to let me alone, are you. You realize what you're getting yourself into? You realize what assessment is?" Assessment is the entry point into SERE (Survive, Evade, Resist, Escape) school and then the Special Forces. They beat you, drug you, starve you, lock you in a dark cell for a week, and blast static and screams from loudspeakers, trying to make you break, trying to see if you can hold up.

Caleb decided to assess anyway, and before assessment he went through a five-week training program called Green Platoon. A lot of carrying logs around and walking through mud. Close quarters combat, weapons, medical. Sticking IVs, chest tubes, shots. How to carry tampons to plug bullet wounds. Sterile. Easy to carry. Great blood stoppers. If somebody got shot, he asked: *Super or regular?* Then a lot of what to do with credit cards, how to deal with travel vouchers. Lots of classroom time. Then it was back outside, more close quarters, standing right across from each other and slugging, learning where to hit for trauma, trying to knock one another unconscious. If the instructor didn't think you were training hard enough, he'd slug on you both and make sure you understood 110 percent. At the end of the week, the instructor put on a foam Red-Man suit and fought the men until they bled. Those weeks were about getting guys to quit.

On the third week the sergeant major lined up all the men. He said, "One of you guys has screwed up and I want you to tell us who it is." Caleb didn't know what was going on. By the looks of it, no one else in the room did either. The sergeant major said *okay then*, walked off, left the men wondering. The next day he came back. It was the same ordeal: lining everybody up, accusing them. "Somebody has done something wrong. Are you going to tell me who it is?"

The room was full of Green Berets, Army Rangers, top-notch guys, and an E-2, a low-ranking guy, just got in the army, hadn't been in the army even a year. The sergeant major looked at the E-2. "Take off your uniform."

This kid, it turns out, went to the store on base and bought all these badges he'd never earned. The Special Forces badge. The airborne wings. The combat badge. All these extra badges. Later he got drunk and put them on his uniform and went to the strip club.

It's Saturday night. The women paw at him, dance for him. The sergeant major is at a table, watching everything.

The E-2 kid cussed the sergeant major. "That's it," he said, "so now I guess I'm kicked out."

The sergeant major said no, you're going to stay in the unit, because it's going to take a while to outprocess you. He stayed for eight months, and they tortured him, harassed him. In close quarters combat, they used him as a dummy. When it was time to learn a knee strike, the sergeant major nailed the kid, and he'd fall down, and he'd get back up. Every day they trained and they trained by him. When Caleb got to the medical portion of Green Platoon, it was January and it was cold and they were out in the woods and this kid was the one who got stuck with IVs. Guys missing veins on purpose.

When Caleb finally told Allyson about his plans to assess, she threatened divorce, telling him that those were the guys who went to hotel rooms and cheated on their wives. Caleb assessed anyway.

When he came home, Allyson wouldn't talk to him. He found his uniform in the trash, buried in a snowfall of tissue. Dog hair and garbage all over the floor. There were no paper towels.

Eventually Allyson suggested he make up for lost time by watching her cheerleading squad at the Georgia Southern men's basketball game. Caleb watched. After the game she told him, "The girls and I are going to Hooters and you can't go. I know how guys are when they go to Hooters."

He'd finally found a job he loved, something he was good at, and the more he loved the army, the less it seemed that Allyson loved him.

He went to Taco Bell to be lonely. He ordered a chalupa extreme, a cheesy double-beef burrito. He spoke to the drive-thru like a confessional, telling it things, things he would never tell anyone else. The face he saw in the yellow window where he received his food was never what he wanted—something beautiful and waiting. But it didn't matter. He ate in the dark, facing the restaurant, so he could see inside.

Nights, he slept in the green-lit back of his truck, someplace new every day, the fast-food chains that broke the dark highway with their haloed light.

He bought a gun and considered killing himself. Back at home, he told Allyson, "This is going to make me sound like a girl, but there's got to be a way to have a relationship besides sex and arguing." She yelled at him, "What do you mean? What do you think a relationship is? It isn't always perfect. Yelling is normal. It helps things."

He got in his car and drove toward nowhere, said he was going to drive until he figured the mess out. While the truck was nagging to start, Allyson was outside in her nightgown, making a scene. He drove all the way back to the base at Hunter, and from there, he drove to SERE school at Fort Bragg, North Carolina.

SERE school was like a prison camp, preparing men for capture, captivity, torture. Once he was running thirty miles during a training exercise with a broken foot, limping, unsure if he could finish. The sergeant came up to him, handed him a thirty-pound weight from his rucksack, and asked Caleb to drop it on his foot. The sergeant's foot. "Now I got a broke foot too," the sergeant said. They continued on their run.

To train, they'd hit the men, kick the men, cover the men with bruises and throw them into a dark room. Someone was always inside, wandering around in the dark. They had to know when they were just a few feet away from the other guy. Then they'd strike.

Caleb made it through SERE school, drugged and beaten within an inch of his life. He was gone a little over a month. That last day he called home and told his father, "I made it. That was the final deal. That was the hardest thing I had to go through." He mentioned the graduation date and hung up.

Next, he called Allyson and told her the same thing. She said she had something important to tell him but she wanted to wait until he came home. Caleb wouldn't hang up the phone.

"You're going to be angry," she said. "You're going to be a dad."

He'd lost thirty pounds from his already-skinny frame. Even his eyes looked smaller. He had yellow bruises on his neck. He ate five green beans for dinner and from that small portion he was full. In a way he was happy about the child because he'd always wanted a family, and so he said nothing at all. He slept for many days and she fed him and he ate and his body re-formed itself.

"Are you still going to leave me?" Allyson asked.

"Yeah, I think so. I can't live this way. You're not who I want to be with."

"I'll change," she said. "I'll change."

Caleb was assigned to the 3rd Battalion, 160th Night Stalkers, at Hunter Army Airfield. Within a week, his pager went off and he was gone to Texas for training at Fort Bliss, four months of flying choppers over the desert. When he got home he took a shower and said harsh words to Allyson. She asked Caleb again if he was going to leave. This time he told her he wasn't. He said he just got home and he wouldn't be going anywhere. When he was gone he'd thought a lot about his daughter and he remembered a promise he'd made to himself, that whatever you do, you stick it out for kids.

The following week Caleb went back to the base to fill out forms for a travel voucher. The soldiers were quiet and drinking coffee and the news played on a television in the corner. CNN showed a plane hitting the first tower, and then another plane hit the second. The colonel walked in and told the men, "I've been on the phone with Washington, prepare to deploy right now." He wouldn't let them leave. He said get your shit and get on the plane. They were to report to duty immediately. Within weeks, Caleb was in Afghanistan, fighting with the 160th Special Ops as part of Operation Enduring Freedom. There wasn't much time to call home. For days, Allyson didn't know where he went.

Caleb came to know the war as green-lit and strange, from the back of a Chinook MH-47D, a seventeen-ton hollow beast strong enough to lift an armored Humvee while keeping speeds up to 155 mph. He was a gunner, pointing the M134 minigun in the dark, searching for tracers. Always in the dark, because the Night Stalkers flew only at night, their helicopters painted black so they would disappear into the dark. The hours they worked in the dark matched closely the American hours of light. When they flew, they stayed close to the ground, the chopper's belly brushing treetops, avoiding ground radar systems. It felt less like flying than moving around things, mountains, buildings, trees, and armies, something elegant, like the flight of bees pollinating pomegranate blossoms.

On his belt Caleb carried a pocket-sized beacon. All of them did. In their pockets, a ten-inch knife for cutting through seat belts and paracord. On their heads, black helmets with a maxillofacial shield to protect from debris, wind back, rotor wash. On their shoulder sleeves, an insignia: a black figure riding a pale horse, carrying a saber. Beneath it, the Night Stalkers' motto: Death Waits in the Dark.

Caleb became part of a crew that manned a Chinook called the *Evil Empire,* tail #146. The Chinook had two rotors, and the aircraft's wide rear opened into a ramp, from which they dropped the Special Forces recon team down the woven nylon ropes deployed on either side, letting them slip to the ground quiet as raindrops down leafstalks. There were stories of men falling, crushing the men below. Sometimes men would fall with straight legs and shatter bone, tibia and fibula.

While Caleb was in Afghanistan, his wife's body grew. She must have worried the child was listening to the silence of the home, that it knew it would be born into a fatherless world.

Caleb was allowed to come home the day before Allyson gave birth. The doctor let him help. He pulled his daughter out. Allyson screamed at him the whole time.

They named their daughter Isabel. At first sight, he feared the girl. He had no idea how to raise one, having grown up among boys. But in the hospital, he held her and she reacted to him and the worry died. Everything he'd ever known in his life, and everything he'd ever loved, he'd either run away from or been kept away from. "And I will never leave you," he said.

Allyson said having the baby ruined her college years because she wasn't skinny like the other girls. Isabel cried through the night. Caleb fed her. Allyson rolled around in bed, covered her ears. Caleb called it postpartum depression. Soon Isabel recognized Caleb's voice and when he spoke she fell asleep to it.

• • •

On his next deployment, after Isabel was born, the *Evil Empire* broke down in the desert of Afghanistan and a radio call came in about how no one was coming to help. It was night. Pitch silent. The unit hunkered. Gunfire flickered in the distance. Forty or fifty Taliban, they guessed, saw the Chinook come down. A hoarse voice over the radio said as much. The chopper was now nothing other than a womb where he would reside and be easily shot, perhaps at close range with great pauses so that he would have time to know the face of his killer. The men didn't speak. They knew they were going to die. The Taliban would either kill him or torture him, but either way, Caleb thought, he didn't want them knowing about Isabel. Since it bothered Caleb to be away from his daughter. He carried a printout photograph of Isabel's smiling face in the pocket of his uniform. Caleb pulled out the picture and looked at his daughter. Then he started eating the picture. He chewed on it. He swallowed it. Eating the picture made him brave. No one, he thought, was going to tell Isabel that her daddy lay down and died in a chopper. That he just gave up. He might die, but if it meant he could live to make it home to see his daughter, then he would be the one biting the esophagus out of a Taliban's throat.

Caleb ate the picture from the bottom up so he could still see Isabel's eyes.

They all stepped out of the chopper and walked across the hot earth and back to base and they never once saw the enemy in their trucks, staring with gun-dark eyes.

Gruesome news about the incident returned to the wives. They'd been gathering in the neighborhood, in each other's homes, talking about what their men were doing. They heard about killings, and perhaps they talked, and the talking made them imagine the killings were done not with guns, or knives, or objects that divided man from enemy—a function of metal and physics—but with hands and with teeth.

And so when Caleb returned, he returned home to a wife who feared him. He stepped into the house and Isabel was in her arms, a boneless shape. Maybe Allyson thought his hands would do something awful. She was white and larger than before, and she wore flannel to hide herself. Caleb opened his arms to receive them and she called him a murderer. Outside, through the open window, he heard the sounds of other fathers mowing lawns, their children playing in the cut grass.

He slept through the day and into the night and in the morning he found a diaper on the bathroom floor, and he was convinced it was the same diaper he saw before he deployed, only now it was ripped up by the dog, spread into pieces, yellow and used. He found his uniform in the trash can.

They slept in different rooms. Allyson didn't trust him around Isabel anymore. Caleb explained that he'd just been through the most traumatic experience of his life. Allyson said he didn't understand what she had to go through being at home by herself.

"I had to take out the trash," she said. "I had to take care of the baby. I had to be alone."

He wondered if she knew he was happy when he left.

He could see faces but he never knew anyone he killed. Most of the time he shot at lights until they stopped flashing. Rarely were there battles. Usually an ammo dump. He held the button down until he couldn't move anymore. Gross motor skills.

Six months later, he was at an Afghan compound. He and his crew of Night Stalkers hovered in the warm night air, waiting for an AC-130 gunship to blow up the guard towers so they could drop off the Special Forces soldiers they sheltered inside the Chinook. The signal to land came through, and Caleb and his buddy Shamus Goare stepped off the rear ramp clearing the way for the soldiers and for the four-wheelers. Everyone called Shamus Goare, "Al Gore." He was thick-cheeked and brown-eyed and he looked too sweet for his job. His life was Chinook #146 and its duties. He was the flight engineer; sometimes working as a gunner, sometimes helping the Special Forces teams down the ropes. On this particular night Caleb and Al Gore stepped outside the chopper's rotor disk and bombs started going off all around them. With their night vision goggles the rounds of explosions turned the world an impossible white. The compound was gone and the guard towers remained. They blew up the wrong part.

The men headed back to the Chinook, and on their way, an object, small and bright like the moon, appeared over the *Evil Empire*. Caleb didn't know what it was or from where it had come. But it came closer. Then he knew. A huge fireball. The flames held something dark, like a pit. A person in the flames. A charred Afghan on a motorcycle, grinning. It hit the ground and the Afghan disappeared into ashes.

The crew returned to the base. They'd taken some heavy fire on the way. Blood was all over the floor of the aircraft. The tie-down rings were covered in severed fingers. Bullets took them clean off.

A few maintenance guys were working their way up the flight path, hauling a big fire hose to spray in the turbine engines and clean all the sand out. When that was done, they would come on the floor of the aircraft and use pressure washers to clean out the dust and dirt. Caleb stepped off and started yelling at them. He looked like hell. He was covered in blood. He was flailing his arms and screaming. "You're not going to come up here," he said. The workers told Caleb it was their job to clean the aircraft. So Caleb snatched the pressure washer and stayed there the rest of the day in the heat and cleaned the blood out of the chopper.

• • •

Caleb's mother collected articles about Iraq and Afghanistan from *USA Today*, the *New York Times*, *Vanity Fair*. She put them in a folder. On a visit home, she showed him the articles. She said, "Is this frivolous? Are people frivolously dying?"

Caleb explained things to his mother. He explained that the bombed Afghan wedding wasn't a wedding at all, and that the press had only thought it was a wedding because that's what the local Afghans had told the press. The locals weren't shooting celebratory fire with Kalashnikovs, he explained, a tradition at Afghan weddings, but were shooting antiaircraft missiles, and that after it was all over the Afghans came and took all the guns away, leaving the women and the children dead and unarmed. "That's all the press had to go by," he said. "If you ask Special Forces what happened, they aren't telling you shit, and by no means would they fly over someone and say, hey, let's kill all these people. And, by the way, do you really think that out of three aircraft of highly trained Special Forces guys, who know they have to write up a report later explaining why they killed everybody, would all three randomly fire onto a village of people and kill all of their women and children?"

Caleb's mother tucked the articles back into the folder. She sat down with her thin limbs and long dark hair. Caleb said, "Guess what, Mom. It was my guys. We did it."

Caleb deployed twice to Iraq and eight times to Afghanistan. In the army, his nickname was Dapper Dan, because no matter what the conditions, after combat, after his helmet had been on his head for days in the Middle Eastern heat, his hair was always immaculate, brushed and molded finely with his favorite gel.

A lot of the war bored him. But sometimes death turned the world into something rare and magnificent. It bonded the men, and pretty soon Caleb felt closer to his unit than he did his wife.

They played together as children. When the *Evil Empire* broke down in the desert, which it often did, they tossed a purple Nerf football to kill time. They threw smoke grenades in a Porta-John. They sang with dumbbells in Delta Forces gyms, "I fucking need you now tonight! I fucking need you now forever!" In Germany, they were drinking at a club and Kip gave the DJ a quiet neck choke—enough to knock him out, keep him down, then drag him behind speakers and tie him with a cord. He switched the techno to Bruce Springsteen's "Born in the USA." Master Sergeant Tre Ponder's wife sent the crew a box of marshmallow Peeps. Tre hated marshmallow Peeps. It was a joke between them, and when the Peeps arrived to the desert, the men used the small yellow birds for target practice. They called the day crew woodchucks because they were always hammering shit at the FOB. Caleb and his buddies went into the woodchuck den one night and started dry humping them. Caleb was running around with a camera. "You better get protection!" The guys grabbed hard helmets, put them on, and started humping again.

At home in Savannah, they all went to Hooters, without their wives, and they signed an army helmet and they hung the helmet on the wall. Nights, they went drinking at Kevin Barry's Irish Pub, a bar in the historic district where the walls are covered in photographs of dead soldiers. Hunter Army Airfield is a ten-minute drive away and all day gray planes fly low over the bar's roof.

The commander of the *Evil Empire* was Major Stephen Reich, and the day he was late for a flight from Texas back to Hunter, the men worried, because he was never late, always by the book. A West Point graduate, your perfect army commander, a roll-up-your-sleeves-and-get-it-done kind of guy. Except that time Caleb said Reich handed Saddam a photo of Jesus and nearly coughed up a lung he was laughing so hard. When Major Reich finally showed up, he was holding a wedding dress, lace and ribbons blowing all over his face. "Can you get this on the aircraft?" Major Reich said. "Don't screw it up." The crew nodded and wove the dress into the *Evil Empire*'s soundproof ceiling so it stayed fresh.

Major Reich was set to marry a woman named Jill Blue whom he met in Forsyth Park in Savannah, when their dogs pressed noses. He asked her out to barbecue. She said she wasn't interested, and he said, oh, come on, what's the worst that could happen?

The wedding dress was her sister's. It arrived at Jill's door in a body bag. That's all the men had.

Four years after the war began, twenty-one-year-old Kip Jacoby showed up to the 3rd Battalion as a helicopter repairman and worked his way up, becoming a Chinook 47D flight engineer, eventually stationed with the *Evil Empire*. Six-foot-two and covered in Alice in Wonderland tattoos—mushrooms, rabbits, cakes—he wore oxblood, steel-toed boots and carried a Glock in his pants. Handsome and morbid in speech, always saying *to hell with this* and *to hell with that*. If you asked how he was doing he'd tell you to go poke his fucking eye out with a spoke. "I don't give a shit about anything," Kip said. "I've got mine." He was the kind of guy you wouldn't want to date your daughter. You either loved him or you hated him. Caleb loved him right away. Bored and on duty, Kip would call Caleb. "Just checking assholes," he'd say, and then hang up. The two of them sat back-to-back in the chopper's tail. Caleb was right gunner, Kip left.

They both chewed Copenhagen snuff and, once, at a desert training exercise near El Paso, they ran out, which to these men was considered a first-rate emergency. Their buddy McCoy said he was getting off base to renew his ID, and he'd bring them both back a can. When McCoy returned, he teased them, said he'd only purchased one. McCoy chewed Red Man himself and laughed at the boys. He sent the single snuff can spinning down the tarmac. Caleb slugged Kip in the face. Kip lunged for Caleb's leg, pulled it back so Caleb's nose staked the asphalt. He was bleeding and stabbed Kip with his boot in the shin. Kip fell in a kneel and Caleb took off chasing the glinting metal, raging for nicotine. He ripped it open and Kip sauntered over. Caleb took a dip, handed it to Kip. He took a dip, handed it back. They were sitting side by side, grinning, the sun an orange smear on the horizon beyond the throb of twin-engine heat.

Caleb and Allyson hadn't been having sex, but one night Allyson woke him and made love to him in such a way that if you'd walked in, not knowing, you might have mistaken it for rage.

Weeks later she stood against the wall. Her nightgown glowed in the evening's light, her body its dark center. She stood rigid, put one foot on top of the other. He saw all of her, touched her stomach to feel his growing son.

"One time?" he said.

He thought they had used a condom. He convinced himself that they definitely had. He convinced himself that she must have gone to the trash to get the condom. He imagined her on the bathroom floor, cinching it shut and then opening it like a wound, wide-legged and pouring it. He on the bed asleep with his back turned, breathing and dreaming.

He punched the wall, and showed her the blood. He tried to explain that he would go to jail if he didn't go to war, and she said that was a decision he had made.

They named their son Isaac. Years passed and his relationship with Allyson deteriorated. He worried his children would get old enough to remember the fighting. He'd promised himself to never let his kids grow up in a house full of bickering, and so Caleb told Allyson he wanted a divorce. He was set to deploy in a month, and she agreed to sign the paperwork while he was gone. But when

Caleb returned from Afghanistan he returned to an empty house, the divorce papers unsigned, and his children gone. Allyson had run off with Cole Boy to Missouri.

The soldiers of #146 heard about what Allyson did and they took Caleb to a strip club to celebrate and mourn. The girls wore sparkles and hoop earrings. Caleb played pool and a girl walked by and he said, "Hey, what are you doing with all your clothes on?" She had long blond hair and fat, wet eyes.

"I'm not a stripper," she said. "I'm a DJ. My name's Krissy." And she walked away.

Before the club closed she asked Caleb if he wanted to go on a date. He told her not really. She said why not. "I don't want to date anyone," he said.

They were sweating and the sweat on their foreheads made them shine like truck oil.

"No strings attached," she said.

Caleb took her number and he called her on Monday and on Tuesday they started dating.

The next time Caleb deployed, he gave Krissy a key to his apartment so she could look after it. When he came home, he found a new bedspread, new lace curtains for the windows. Framed photos of them hung on the wall. He found a diamond engagement ring in his shirt drawer. She'd used his credit card to buy it. "Don't you want to be with me?" she said.

The dreams began when the death toll rose and the nights warmed in the summer before his friends would die. The foresight, the eerie vibes—for a long time he'd write it off, say it was coincidence, but then the other guys in his unit would see the same thing. At military briefings, he'd stare at blueprints, and then he'd see it: two guys with AKs behind the second door on the left. Sure enough, they'd be waiting for him. This happened over and over. People began to call him psychic. Soon the officers had him lead the briefings; telling the soldiers what he thought would happen.

He saw the *Evil Empire* bursting into flames, everyone dying. In the dream the Night Stalkers are flying through the mountains looking for a place to land, and when there's no good place to land, the pilot holds a hover. The pilot can't see anything going on in the back, so there's a guy hanging off the ramp, talking on the radio: *Come back one, hold her right. Come back left, hold back two.* And the pilot is listening to this voice. It's the inflection of the voice. Everybody is talking but nobody is stepping on one another. It's a critical time. They're lining up for a fast rope landing. Caleb throws the rope off the ramp and the men start sliding down at ten or fifteen feet off the ground. That's when the firing begins. They're stopped. They're hovering. They're at their most critical point. All their guns are hanging off the side. The rounds are bouncing off the electrical panels and the helicopter peels over and they get hit from the back by a rocket.

You know those falling dreams? The ones where you're in an elevator and you're falling but you never hit the ground—you're just falling, falling?

Caleb can't see anything. He can only see flashes. He can see colors. Everything is blurred out, like if you put goggles on your face and rubbed the front with Vaseline.

In the dream, he's lying there on his side, and the aircraft is turning over and everybody is screaming.

"Kip," Caleb yells, "Kip, buddy, can you get out? I'm pinned down. I can't move." Caleb is on his side, peering into the smoke.

Then he hears it: "Caleb, I'm burning, man. I'm *fucking* burning."

Months before their next deployment, in the spring of 2005, Kip was heading home from the base, driving this old sloppy car, with broken wipers and no insurance. He was on his way to see his new girlfriend, Kristina, a twenty-year-old he'd met at a restaurant in Savannah. When the two met, Kristina was working as a hostess and Kip had been dating the bartender. Kristina thought maybe Kip was a little bipolar. He was loud and passionate and didn't care what anyone thought. Kristina and Kip started flirting and the flirting got out of control, and right away things got serious and they moved in together. Kristina went out to bars with the crew. She was a good drinker, had no problem keeping up. Kip always moved from one woman to the next, but Kristina was different.

Kip was in a rush to see her but Caleb wouldn't let him drive off the base, not without insurance.

"I don't care " Kip said. Kip opened his shirt. He had a new tattoo of the *Evil Empire*.

Caleb tossed Kip the keys to his own truck. "Don't fuck it up. Have a nice weekend." Kip leaned his head out the window and told Caleb to hang on a second. "We're going to die in that fucking desert, aren't we?"

Caleb folded his arms, dug at the dirt with his shoe. He told Kip to shut his face.

Al Gore had an old Camaro that wouldn't run. He'd get frustrated, drink beer, try to make it work, then get more drunk and pissed off. A meaty guy. Loved hot rods. Never real bossy. Never large and in charge, but there were a few times in his life when he'd get stuck and stubborn. The same month Kip showed Caleb his new tattoo of the *Evil Empire,* Caleb was helping Al Gore repair the Camaro. They were trying to fix the temp switch on the fan because the engine kept overheating, and so Caleb tried to wire it so the fan ran all the time, and in the middle of all this fixing, Al Gore turned to Caleb and said, "I'm going to die in that desert."

• • •

In May 2005, a month before their deployment, Caleb called Allyson in Missouri and told her about the dreams. "I need to see the kids. I'm not coming home from this one."

Allyson screamed at him, hung up the phone, called Caleb's superior, First Sergeant Perez, and told him that her ex-husband ought to be put in a mental institution because he was having these crazy dreams.

Perez called Caleb into his office, sat him down, and asked if all of this was true—the dreams, the visions. Caleb shook his head. He wouldn't tell him anything.

Major Reich had an office across the hall from Perez and overheard everything. He told the men to get into his office.

"First Sergeant Perez, you can leave." He told Caleb to close the door.

"So," he said, "are you going to tell me about these crazy dreams?" Caleb shook his head. Major Reich leaned forward and said, "Because I've been having the same dreams."

Major Reich pulled the unit together in his office and offered them the chance to back out. "Your aircraft has been in more firefights than anybody's," he said. "You guys are all the divorced angry ones. You guys always volunteer for everything. Why don't you sit this one out, do the next rotation."

Caleb and Kip were the main guys in that aircraft; they'd deployed for years together—sleeping and eating in that aircraft. They knew every inch of it. Al Gore. Mike Russell. They all knew. They all had the same dreams—their chopper's tail number—#146—disappearing into a curtain of flames. One by one, the men stared at each other. Too brute, too proud. Macho men. No one was going to say anything. No one was going to say, I'm having these crazy dreams. They tap-danced around it.

The crew deployed in May 2005, and in June they were in the shadow of the Hindu Kush mountains, in the Kunar province of eastern Afghanistan, the most violent region in the most violent season of the war. Hindu Kush means "Hindu-killer." The word *kush* derives from the Berber for "to slaughter" or "to kill." When the Hindu slaves traveled from India to the Muslim courts of central Asia, the mountains killed them in hordes. In their weather and their extremes; their low, warm valleys and high, cold peaks; their deep, burrowing network of caves, they have seen more violence than any other region in Afghanistan.

The mission was called Operation Red Wings and the goal was to kill or capture Taliban Ahmad Shah, leader of an insurgent group called the Mountain Tigers. The Night Stalkers were going to insert four Navy SEALs in the same location where the Afghan people warred against the British who arrived in 1839, the Soviets who arrived in 1980, and the Americans who arrived in 2001. The same mountains where, in April 1985, a tribe of Afghans ambushed a hundred Russian Special Operations soldiers and cut their throats.

Period of darkness June 27, Major Stephen Reich and Captain Matthew Brady, platoon leader of the Night Stalkers of Bravo Company, gathered in Bagram for a mission brief.

Caleb's crew would fly to Asadabad and waited as part of a Quick Reaction Force, a rescue team, in case anything happened to the SEALs.

At six in the evening, at sundown, another Chinook carried the four-man SEAL team, including Lieutenant Mike Murphy and Petty Officers Danny Dietz, Matt Axelson, and Marcus Luttrell, into the Hindu Kush, traveling at one hundred knots, flying close to the ground, and dropped them off on the side of a mountain called Sarwalo Sar. The Chinook hovered at twenty feet, and the recon team fast-roped to the ground. There was no moon. They crawled into an area of fern and cedar and dead upright trees.

At Jalalabad the operations team monitored the SEALs, and

once their positions were secure, SEAL team commander Eric Kristensen shipped operations back over to Bagram.

The SEALs rested in the mountains during the daylight.

The four SEALs had been walking through the woods when an Afghan jumped out of the trees and came at Marcus Luttrell with an ax. Axelson had a gun at the Afghan's head before the ax could chop. Two more men and a kid appeared from the trees, followed by goats. The herders had no guns. The soldiers told them to sit still. Lieutenant Murphy said they had three options: kill the goat herders and toss the bodies over the cliff, kill the goat herders and bury the bodies, or let the herders go.

Dietz said he didn't care. Axelson voted to kill. It was up to Luttrell. He voted to let the men go home.

The herders, set free, must have run off and told the Taliban, because hours later Shah's men chased the SEALs down the mountain in a parade of fire: machine guns, AK-47s, rocket-propelled grenades.

Danny Dietz died first, shot four times. It was the fifth bullet that killed him. Murphy found him and decided it was a good time to radio the base for backup. But he couldn't get reception so he crawled to an open area, in full view of the Taliban. He said we're dying out here. A bullet entered his back. Blood spurted on the radio. He hung up. Murphy stumbled to a rock face for cover. Luttrell followed his screams but they faded before he made it to the body. Luttrell found Axelson in a hollow, half his skull blown off, eye sockets full and dark with blood.

Captain Brady hadn't been sleeping long when the maintenance officer walked into his bunker and told him to wake up. He said he'd been in the operations center and the SEALs had been compromised. The evacuation situation and requirements were unclear.

Caleb woke up to the sound of Captain Brady gathering the platoon, talk of a new mission. Lieutenant Robert Long, assistant operations commander, notified the men that he'd received a distress call from the SEALs. The Night Stalkers waited for orders. A second call came in from the SEALs, but they didn't need to say much because Lieutenant Long heard the sounds of rocket-propelled grenades and automatic weapons and maybe an eighty-two-millimeter mortar system. The call went dead. No one spoke. Lieutenant Long cracked his knuckles. Forty-five minutes passed. He didn't have the authority to launch the rescue team, so he waited on the SEAL liaison team, who made rushed calls to Bagram and waited on the authorities there. It was a mess. Caleb and his crew stood ready. They were at a wood guard shack at the east end of the strip.

At three thirty in the afternoon, the rescue mission was approved. Caleb and the rest of the crew prepared three Apache Attack Birds and two MH-47 Chinooks, including #146, the *Evil Empire*.

Sergeant Marcus Muralles stepped on the aircraft. He wasn't supposed to be on the flight but the other medic had an injured leg. Muralles had been packing to get home to celebrate the tenth birthday of his daughter Anna.

Al Gore stepped on the flight and took a seat in the back of the Chinook. He was the guy who was going to help the Special Forces rescue teams get down the ropes. Gore wasn't supposed to be on the flight either, but he'd kicked off another soldier who had a wife and two kids. Al Gore was single, and he never married because he figured he had a good chance of dying. He always volunteered to go on dangerous missions so that the soldiers with wives and kids wouldn't.

Captain Matthew Brady stepped on the flight. The blades were turning, and he was putting on his football gear when Major Reich walked up to him, peered inside, and said, "What's your plan, Brady?"

Brady started explaining the mission, how he was going to enter the mountains and save the stranded SEALs.

"No, you're not," Major Reich said. "Get your shit and get off the chopper. You didn't do anything wrong. Just get your shit and get off."

Brady got his shit and got off.

The night before, Major Reich had sent his wife an e-mail saying he'd had a dream, but it wasn't about the *Evil Empire,* it was about her. He said that in the dream Jill Blue was watching over him and they were together and he was happy and safe. Thank you for your presence, he wrote, even in a dream. They e-mailed every day. A few days before he'd written to tell her he loved her more than anyone he'd ever loved, and that they loved each other in a way that was beyond love and he wished he had a word for it.

Caleb was preparing to get on board the chopper when Tre Ponder, the one who hated marshmallow Peeps, told Caleb he wouldn't be flying this mission. Tre was in Afghanistan to train men, not to fly, but when the opportunity to fly came up, he took it. Tre was Caleb's superior and Caleb had no choice in the matter. There was nothing he could do.

Caleb waited in the rotor wind. He was watching, moving around. The men sealed themselves behind helmets and doors and guns.

That's when Kip strolled up to Caleb, completely sober in tone, and told him he needed to make a promise. "When we die, buddy," he said, "it's not your fault. Don't ever think it's your fault. You're going home and you're going to get out. You've been chosen for a bigger mission. You've been here longer than anyone else and you've already paid your price. This war is just the half of it. It's just the beginning. You don't need to pay the price here anymore."

Caleb tried to interrupt. He was Kip's superior. It was Caleb's job to talk, and Kip's job to listen, but it was completely the other way around for this conversation.

"Fuck," Kip said. "You shut the fuck up." He told Caleb to take care of Kristina, the only girl he'd ever loved. "She'll probably end up screwing a Ranger, but that's okay." His blond hair tangled in the rotor wind. "This war is just the half of it. It's just the beginning." He shivered and spoke Bible words and filled his cheeks with Copenhagen. He mentioned something about building vehicles. He talked about Caleb going home to Georgia and falling in love. "You go home," he said, "and you save lives." Kip tapped the ground with his foot. "Promise me," he said, "you'll come back to get our bodies. Get our bodies out of this country. I hate this fucking country."

Kip walked back to the chopper. Behind him, a small string of chew on the tarmac, a little glimmering part left behind. Kip turned around. There was one more thing. "If you reenlist, Caleb, I will come back to Georgia, and I will haunt you."

The first rescue chopper took off heavy with men—too many men—a dangerous load. It stopped in Jalalabad and the *Evil Empire* swept past, hauling sixteen men, eight Navy SEALs and eight Night Stalkers. They outran the Apache Attack birds that flew fifty feet above the ground, and entered the Hindu Kush, alone.

At the same spot where the SEALs were dropped, the Chinook hovered. The rear ramp opened. The Night Stalkers prepared the fast ropes for a second insertion. One of Ahmad Shah's men watched from a mountain crevice. He loaded a rocket-propelled grenade, aimed it at the aircraft, said *Allahu akbar*, "God is great," and fired. The rocket flew through the Chinook's open back, past the men's heads, directly into the transmission, turning the metal into a liquid that consumed them. The chopper erupted. Men shot off the loading ramp. Bodies burned. The *Evil Empire* keeled, nose up, and fell fifty feet to the ground, rolling down the mountain, exploding. A huge fireball.

The other Chinook circled the downed chopper, moving through smoke plumes, and thunderclouds. The command center said hold off—*wait.* In fifteen minutes they said, *come back.*

Kip Jacoby was dead. Al Gore was dead. Steve Reich and Marcus Muralles and Tre Ponder and Corey Goodnature were dead. Mike Russell and Chris Scherkenbach. Everyone burned alive. Eight Night Stalkers and eight Navy SEALs. At the time, it was the worst Special Forces disaster in the history of the war.

Captain Brady took over as commanding officer of Bravo Company. He had to generate a new rescue team, a new security force. Mobilize. Decide on the correct insertion point, the combat capability mix. Get new guys onto an aircraft. They attempted three times, but each time failed. They couldn't insert. They lost visibility to rain and black clouds. On the third attempt, they quit. They didn't want to lose more men. Let this blow over, they said, and we'll try again at nightfall.

No one knew that three of the SEALs were already dead. That they died before the *Evil Empire* took flight. The fourth, Marcus Luttrell, didn't linger when he saw the chopper explode. He'd seen the last of his friends die. Luttrell loped off into the woods, bracing against the pain of bullet wounds, cracked vertebrae, shrapnel in the leg, dehydration, and a head wound. The Taliban stalked him through the night.

Caleb's enlistment was up. His eardrums ached from all the mortar explosions. He jumped on the next Freedom Flight home.

On the ground at Hunter, they told him everyone was dead.

Get our bodies out of this country, I hate this fucking country.

He flew back to Afghanistan to get their bodies.

SEAL teams and Rangers were already climbing the mountain, searching for survivors, trying to get the bodies. They knew everybody was dead, but to verify death you have to have a corpse. It took days. The enemy had rushed in. They'd looted the SEALs. It was hot. Smelled like charred flesh. Everything was blown up by a minigun. The rescuers knew who was who by where the burned flesh piled in the aircraft. Later there were DNA tests. They found a dog tag engraved with inspirational quotes. They found Major Reich's wedding ring in the troop commander's seat. He wasn't supposed to be wearing it, but he'd kept it hidden under his flight glove.

The rescuers scooped the remains into body bags. Just pieces—bones and flesh. Wasn't much left. Their bodies went to the Bagram mortuary. Caleb waited for Kip. He doesn't remember how long he waited. Maybe three or four days. Kip went in a box and then in a plane and they flew together over the Atlantic to Dover, Delaware, where all the bodies return.

From Dover, Marcus Muralles went to Arlington. Shamus Goare to Danville, Ohio. Stephen Reich to Panama City, Florida.

Kip's body went to Savannah. Caleb drove after Kip, looking up, seeking the plane's small black shape against the blue sky.

Caleb waited at the offices at Hunter for news of Kip's funeral. One of the Special Ops guys, the one they called the jokester, walked up to Caleb. "You got out of that one pretty easily," he said. "You fucking killed them. They're all dead because of you." Maybe he wasn't serious but Caleb knocked him in the face with a chair anyway. He wanted to kill him and he was trying to kill him. Blood spraying all over the office floor. Caleb wouldn't stop. Six men pulled him off.

Everywhere he went, Caleb heard it, over and over again: *You killed them, Caleb. Why are you the one to be living?*

Caleb was thinking about his promise to take care of Kip's girlfriend, Kristina. Caleb had direct orders not to tell Kristina about Kip's death. The Casualty Assistance Officers would tell her first. They said he'd end up in protective custody. But Caleb didn't care. They met in Forsyth Park. "I know," she said. "I mean, I didn't really know. But I knew." She'd heard on NPR that a helicopter crashed and the helicopter they described was the *Evil Empire.*

Caleb told Kristina that if there was anything of Kip's she wanted to keep, then she needed to make it disappear because otherwise the military would find it and take it.

Two days later Kip's uncle called Kristina to tell her that her boyfriend was dead.

Kristina wanted to know why Kip's parents didn't call.

Guilt-stricken, the uncle said. Traumatized. They couldn't deal with it. They threw their hands in the air and told the army to deal with it. And the way the army deals with it is that you get it done and you get it done now.

Kip's uncle asked her a few questions: Where did Kip want to be buried? Did he want to be cremated? What kind of coffin did he want?

Kristina said she didn't know because she and Kip never sat around and talked about dying.

She was twenty. She said that the fact that her live-in boyfriend was never coming home was a lot for a twenty-year-old to deal with.

Later Kristina thought maybe the funeral should be at Arlington.

Kip's mother told her that wouldn't be happening because the army killed her son and she hated the army.

Kristina waited for the knock of the Casualty Assistance Officers. Meanwhile she hid Kip's steel-toed boots and Glock in the trunk of her car. She piled his clothes on the living room floor while her father sat on the couch, mother on the chair, and they watched while Kristina folded. She held each piece of clothing to her nose so as not to forget Kip's smell. All the clothes smelled like him—the sweat, the deodorant, the detergent, and the scents he used to cover these scents.

Three days later, the officers arrived at her house just as Caleb said they would. It was seven in the morning and the sky was white and the room was cold. Kristina was still asleep on the couch, wearing jeans and a T-shirt. In the days following Kip's death, she preferred the couch to her bed—using a torn spot where some foam broke through as a pillow.

The men raided the house. They opened drawers. They took everything that belonged to Kip. Clothes, guns, computers. Everything. They didn't say two words to Kristina. They brought a chaplain and he walked up to Kristina and said, do you need to talk? She said, *I'm fine*. The men packed Kip's things in heavy plastic bags and brought them to his parents' house in Pompano Beach. They put the bags on the front steps. Delivered them like lunch.

Kip's father, Steve, told Caleb he wanted an open casket at the funeral. Caleb said that wouldn't be happening. Steve said, "I want to see my son. My son is dead." Caleb shook his head. "There'll be no open casket."

Steve wouldn't listen. "I want an open casket." Caleb had to drive Steve to the morgue to convince him otherwise. He unzipped the body bag and told Steve to look. Kip was just pieces—bones and skin and ash. There were parts missing. There was a large chunk of femur.

"We're not doing an open casket."

Steve said, "Okay." He was weeping into his hands. "I get it. I get it."

Kristina found out from Caleb that Kip's funeral would be in Miami at a place called Forest Lawn, nine hours south. She found out the day before. Caleb and his army friend Denis drove Kristina to Florida, the whole way, with air-conditioning and bad music and stops at fast-food chains and gas stations full of inflatable sea animals and stacks of purple chewing gum.

When they arrived at the funeral, Kristina wasn't allowed inside. She wasn't on the guest list. She'd never been close to Kip's parents and they never put her on the list. Caleb tried to figure out what was going on. Steve said he lost his only son and wanted to have a private funeral. He didn't mean any harm. Kristina waited in the car. The family didn't want any soldiers to show up except Caleb and Denis. No military honors. Nothing. They didn't want anyone at the funeral wearing a uniform.

The priest said few words. Kip was in in the same box he was shipped home in. Nobody ordered a casket.

Kip's mother wasn't there. Steve left in the middle of the ceremony.

When Kristina got home to Savannah she found a letter from Kip in her mailbox. I'll be coming home in twenty-eight days, he said.

After the funeral, Caleb drove to the Blue Star Memorial in Savannah. The ground was covered in bricks inscribed with the names of dead soldiers. Caleb bought a brick for Kip and set it in the ground. Next to Kip, Caleb put down a brick for himself. A brick means you're dead. Caleb liked being there next to his friend.

When the army organized a memorial service in Savannah they gave Kip the Purple Heart, the Bronze Star, the Service Medal, the Good Conduct Medal, the Air Medal, the Combat Action Badge.

After Kip's parents received a military check for his life insurance, they divorced. Caleb heard the money went to a new car and gambling in Vegas; silicone breasts for the mom.

Kip's ex-wife was a stripper from Florida. Caleb had this story about how Kip and the stripper bought a place together after the wedding and when he returned from his first deployment in Afghanistan, her things were in boxes. She left a note saying she went to visit her family, but she never came back. Kip and Caleb had dug through the boxes. They found homemade porn videos of her fucking. Kip forgot to change his will, so the money was still in the name of the stripper. Kristina didn't get anything.

Jill Blue learned that her husband was dead while she was at work at her father's law firm in Panama City, Florida. The chaplain and the officers showed up. She told them to be quiet. She sprinted out the door. They chased her all the way home. After she let them inside, she grabbed one of the men by his uniform, pushed him in the laundry room, and said, *I know, I know. Don't say anything. I know.*

She keeps Steve Reich's Night Stalker helmet in the living room. It looks like a helmet built for deep-sea diving or space exploration. She was disappointed the army didn't let her keep the night vision goggles. When Halloween comes around, sometimes she puts on a fancy dress, slips the helmet over her head, and wanders the streets, masquerading as the dead.

The parents of Marcus Muralles, when they learned of their son's death, requested that the street names in their neighborhood no longer be named after trees but after dead soldiers. Elm. Maple. Oak. Why not the dead? Now his mother can see the sign for Muralles Street outside her window, just across Interstate 74, into the Marin Estates apartment complex. Sometimes they go visit the street. She takes pride in picking up litter on the street named for her son. Because Muralles was buried far from Ohio, in Arlington Cemetery, she's never been able to see his grave. Instead she hired a woman to take photos of the grave and she looks at these photos instead.

Leslie Ponder covered Tre Ponder's grave site with brightly colored marshmallow Peeps.

Shamus Goare had a little brother named Cory who worked

at an industrial factory. One year and two months after the Chinook crashed, Cory died. A machine pinched his head. The brothers were born thirteen months apart and they died fourteen months apart. Their family called the two of them mashed potatoes and gravy. Cory's wife thinks he wasn't paying attention because he was too sad about Shamus's death. Judy blames Marcus Luttrell for not killing the goat herders. She mentions that her son's body wasn't burned up as badly as the others.

Because a crew card had been mailed back to Savannah listing the names of every soldier on the *Evil Empire,* Captain Brady's wife believed her husband was dead. For forty-eight hours she lived in a soft, mournful world. The card was never updated with Major Reich's name.

When Brady returned home from the war in September 2005, he found an e-mail from Jill Blue in his in-box. When Major Reich went on dangerous missions, his e-mails rerouted to Brady. The e-mail was addressed to Major Reich. It was the only e-mail. He didn't want to open it.

Stephen, tell me you are okay? Tell me it wasn't you? I need you now more than ever. I love you.

Some members of Captain Brady's platoon got out of the military. Some stayed and served and were killed. Some stayed and saw their buddies killed and then got out because they were thinking: When's my time?

At the SEAL 160 Ride, a memorial service honoring the fallen soldiers of Operation Red Wings, Captain Brady saw Jill Blue. It was the first time since Steve Reich died. He reached his arms out and held her. She said nothing.

"I just want you to know," he said, "that Major Reich died to save the wounded, and to bring our men home, and he did it out of a sense of duty and he will always be memorialized and remembered for his courage."

"I don't care what you think," she said. "I don't care that my husband tried to save all those people. In fact, I think your motto is pretty stupid. *Night Stalkers Don't Quit*. What does that mean to me? How does that help me? Is that what you guys do? Do you guys just keep doing things until you're all dead? Because now my husband is dead. He's dead because of *you*."

That's when Captain Brady started having terrible dreams. No dream bothered him as much as this dream. The one he had on the fifth of August 2011.

In the dream Major Reich stepped aboard a Chinook helicopter and he paused to look back at Brady. Then he started to burn. Major Reich was bursting into flames. His lips peeled back like wilted petals. "Brady," Reich said, "I've got this one."

The next day a Chinook MH-47, the same chopper as the *Evil Empire*, carrying a Quick Reaction Force in the Wardak province of Afghanistan, was shot down. Thirty-eight men on board died, surpassing the death toll of Operation Red Wings.

Sometimes Brady walks down the street and a stranger's face will shift and morph and become the face of Major Stephen Reich.

After the crash, Caleb was still dating Krissy, and she found him sometimes shaking on the floor, watching the crash all over again in his dreams: the choking gray-black smoke swirling with the voices of Kip and Al Gore. *Kip, buddy, can you get out?* Caleb was always looking for Kip. *I'm burning, man. I'm fucking burning.*

Caleb asked Kip: why am I still alive when everybody else is dead? Kip led Caleb down a dark stairwell. He wrote Scripture on the walls in cursive, *You were slain, and have redeemed us to God by your blood out of every kindred, and tongue, and people, and nation; and have made us to our God kings and priests.*

Krissy had enough of the dreams, the visions. The bodies ripped apart. Dreams where there was no more blood because it's all in the dirt next to you. Dying in the worst ways. The *Evil Empire* in their bedroom at night, perfuming the air.

"You see Kip too, don't you?" Caleb asked. Krissy shook her head.

Caleb had his eyes turned sightlessly toward the light. Krissy woke him. "Am I so horrible you have to sleep in the garage?" she said.

She got up and dug under the clothes where their engagement ring still sat untouched, and found a gun. It was a little white gun. A birthday present from Caleb. She walked downstairs. The afternoon sun poured through the unclean windows. He said she put the gun to her head.

He told her to put the gun down.

The only way he could stop her from shooting herself, he decided, was to put a gun to his own head.

Caleb ran outside. Krissy chased after him. He got in his pickup truck, shut the door, and locked her out. It smelled like rain. He opened the glove compartment and pulled out his gun, put it in his mouth. She stood at the window, looking inside with blue eyes. "I can't live with you this way." They both had guns to their heads. Birds moved around in the trees. Finally Krissy lowered her gun so Caleb wouldn't shoot.

Everywhere he went, he saw them, their burned bodies, watching him.

These were the days after the war.

PART II

WE KILL OURSELVES
BECAUSE WE ARE HAUNTED

I met Sergeant Caleb Daniels in a parking lot off Lake Allatoona in Georgia three years after Kip Jacoby's death.

The sky was desolate warm and white. A dock frothed with roped-up boats and water licked the sand, leaving a rim of yellow, glistening foam. It was quiet for summer, no growling motors or tires breaking over gravel, just the sound of a slow breeze. A bird wetted its beak in the stomach of a dead squirrel.

When I arrived Caleb wasn't there—nobody was. He showed up thirty minutes late, driving a burgundy Chevrolet with rust-eaten sides, wearing a button-up shirt, one-hundred-fifty-dollar jeans, and cowboy boots with a two-inch lift. His stubble sparkled like bits of sand. Six-foot-one. Sideburns thick as duct tape. Everything about him was pale but for his hair, which was black and oiled so that its blackness shined. Nowhere longer than a fingernail. He spit chew on the pavement and it steamed.

Over the phone Caleb told me he planned to buy abandoned factories across Georgia and hire a veterans-only workforce to rebuild old combat vehicles for humanitarian and civilian use;

turning the waste products of war into something that would give life instead of destroy it. The veterans would have work if they needed work. They'd have a community if they needed a community. The profits would feed into suicide counseling programs for soldiers, which, I later found out, was a Christian exorcism camp. Caleb would run it. There was a small news clip about him in the *Statesboro Herald.*

The factory he wanted to buy stood alone in the center of a field in southeast Georgia. It was a drab metal thing made grand by the space around it. He'd been building things all his life, unfinished things, trying to make them whole. Caleb relished it, the lives he'd save, the days breaking back, hauling trucks, orchestrating the rise of steel beams. Already he carried notebooks and blueprints; drove a truck with a six-cylinder engine. At night, in his dreams, he saw the vehicles he wanted to build and he gave them names: Brute, Savage, Aggressor. He befriended a broker in Kennesaw, a large bald man named Buck, and convinced Buck to help him write a business proposal for the company. They determined a start-up cost of two and a half million dollars.

It was 2008, and the Department of Veterans Affairs had been caught withholding statistics on veteran suicide from the public. When CBS News began an investigation into the rates, the head of mental health at the VA said, "The research is ongoing. There is no epidemic in suicide in the VA, but suicide is a major problem." Then he sent an e-mail to his media adviser with the subject line "Not for the CBS News Interview Request." He wrote that there were a thousand suicide attempts per month within the VA. He wrote *Shh!*

Around eighteen veterans were killing themselves every day.

Private Jonathan Schulze, who lost fifty-one members of his unit in Ramadi and Fallujah in 2004, returned home and told his parents he wanted to die. He was number 26 on the waiting list to be admitted to the VA in St. Cloud, Minnesota, when the police found him hanging by an electrical cord in his parent's basement.

Army specialist Timothy Israel, who had been awarded a Purple Heart after being wounded by a roadside bomb, hung himself with the drawstring of his pants in a jail cell in Elwood, Indiana.

Russell Dwyer, a former platoon sergeant and cavalry scout instructor at Fort Knox, shot his wife in the head in their front yard in Colorado Springs, and then he lay down beside her and shot himself. She was facedown, he chose faceup.

Lieutenant Corporal Jeffrey Lucey, who served in a company responsible for transporting Iraqi prisoners of war, hanged himself with a garden hose in the cellar of his family's home.

Private First Class Stephen S. Sherwood, a veteran of the casualty-heavy battle for Ramadi, shot his wife five times in the head and neck with a pistol, then took a shotgun to his own head.

Sergeant Lisa Morales said, in an interview in the *New York Times*, that she reenlisted because she wanted to go back to Iraq so that the Iraqis would shoot her for what she'd done.

Private Walter Rollo Smith, a Marine Corps reservist who'd marched to Baghdad in the first invasion returned home to his twin duplex in Tooele, Utah, made love to the mother of his children, washed her in the bath, pushed her head underwater to rinse out the soap, and held it there gently until she died. When I called Private Smith's attorney to see if I could visit Smith in jail, the attorney said I could not. "Everyone already knows he's suffering from PTSD."

Caleb was eager to tell his story, but most were not. The first person I called was the mother of Joshua Omvig, whose son is considered the first suicide of the Iraq war. She had a home in Grundy Center, Iowa, half an hour from where I lived, in a spread of quiet cornfields. Specialist Joshua Omvig of the 339th MP Company shot himself in December 2005, three days before Christmas. What happened was he handed his mother a suicide note that she thought was a Christmas list. She set it aside. She'd look at it later. There were dishes to be done. She returned to the sink and started washing. Joshua was in his bedroom, changing into his uniform, the one he wore on an eleven-month deployment in Iraq. When he was fully dressed, Joshua walked past his mother and headed outside. The suicide note was still unread. Still on the counter. Joshua climbed into the family truck, locked all the doors, pulled out the 9mm he'd stashed in the glove compartment, and brought it to his head. Joshua's mother was reading the note. She ran outside, arms flailing, and stopped beside the passenger window. He angled the gun just slightly so he wouldn't kill his mother. He was twenty-three years old. "You don't understand," he said. "I've been dead ever since I left Iraq."

Two years after Joshua's suicide I called his mother. She didn't want to talk to me. She had this quiz she gave all the newspaper guys before she let them ask her questions. I told her I wasn't a newspaper guy. She said it didn't matter. What's post-traumatic stress? What's happening to the brain? She wanted medical terms, and scientific reasoning, and I gave her the answers I knew. She said to go read the *DSM,* the *Diagnostic and Statistical Manual of Mental Disorders,* and get back to her. The *DSM* is the official handbook of mental illness and disorder in the United States. In terms of treatment, nothing's a disorder unless the *DSM* says it's a disorder. I had in fact read the *DSM*'s classification criteria for post-traumatic stress and what I knew was that the *DSM* revises its definition of war-related trauma in every edition, and has been revising it since its first installment. It wasn't until 1980, in *DSM-III*, that the term *post-traumatic stress disorder* appeared as an operational diagnosis. To be diagnosed with PTSD, one must have experienced a traumatic event, and *DSM-III* defines a traumatic event as one outside the range of usual human experience. The DSM does not define usual human experience.

I said I was very sorry for what happened to her son. The mother paused and then asked whether I'd fallen all the way to the bottom of hell and stayed for a while and then come back to earth again. She said that unless you've been to the bottom of hell and come back you couldn't understand young Joshua's blood splattering on the windshield anyway.

When I called a woman named April Somdahl, the half sister of twenty-six-year-old Sergeant Brian Rand, a marine who believed he was being followed night after night by the ghost of the Iraqi man he'd killed, she told me a story about the day Brian was in Iraq and she was in North Carolina and they were talking on Yahoo! Chat and Brian said he needed April's advice. He said there was a guy out in the sand, and he'd been out there for hours and he wouldn't come inside.

"Well, what's he doing?"

Brian sent his buddy Chris out to check on the guy. When Chris returned, he stood in the middle of the room and stared at the floor.

"So what'd he say?"

"Remember those people in the convoy that blew up earlier today?" Chris said. "Well, they blew up into billions of pieces. He's looking for them because he thinks he needs to collect a fragment of their body to take home and give to their family."

"Bring him inside," April said. "I'll talk to him."

Chris brought the soldier inside. He sat him down in front of the computer.

"Hi, hey," April said. "How you doing? I'm out here in North Carolina—"

"—BILLIONS OF PIECES! Billions and billions and billions. I gotta find one."

"Now listen," April said. "That's not very nice, to pick up a piece of someone and give it back to their family, is it? I think that would freak them out."

"No, no. They have to have a piece of them. I just need one little piece. It could be anything."

"Those men are dead," April said. "You're not going to bring them back. The families will have a funeral for them. If you bring a piece of their bodies back to their families you could hurt them. You don't want to hurt them, do you?"

The soldier said nothing.

"Are you going home soon?"

"Billions of pieces! Billions of pieces! Billions and billions and billions and billions. Billions and billions."

He kept saying it, billions and billions, over and over.

"Please stop," April said.

The soldier stopped.

"There may be billions of pieces of them all over the earth, but do you know those pieces will sink into the earth and they will form new soil or even fossils and they will become part of the world again? That was only their bodies. Their souls had already passed on into heaven. They are probably looking down on you right now, thinking how crazy you are."

The soldier said nothing.

"I'll tell you what: when I die, you can take my body and throw it over my neighbor's fence."

"Really?" he said.

I wanted to talk to veterans and the families of veterans for the same reason that many were telling me I could not talk to them. That as soon as we say words like *PTSD* or *trauma* we have permission to ignore the problem because we think we understand it. It wasn't so much that the familiar narratives weren't working, it was there appeared to be no narrative at all.

At the end of the phone conversation with April, she asked, "Was *that* PTSD?"

When I drove into Georgia I called Caleb and asked where we should meet. He said he was busy running errands, trying to find a boat engine for a girl named DeeAnne whose husband had just died of a heart attack. "It's a piece-of-shit houseboat," he explained, "but she won't give it up. It was where her husband liked to go to think. This guy was huge. He ate so much food that one day he pretty much just fell over and died. Just last week she bought a new engine for ten grand, and guess what? Two days later it broke."

Caleb knew a guy in a town called Dalton selling boat parts. "Consider this," he told me. "Once I asked my marine buddy Max to come help me fix vehicles. He didn't want to meet me. He was on his way to drill. But I convinced him anyway. Guess what? The guys he was gonna ride with got stuck behind a Greyhound, and a big bus tire flew off and smashed their window. They ended up in the ditch." The way he told it, he was a kind of talisman against death.

I left my car in the parking lot and stepped into Caleb's truck. Tobacco dust lined every inch of it. The worn leather scratched my thighs. Caleb looked a bit feverish. At the same time, on the edge of recovery.

We drove with open windows, feeling the air. He looked at me and sniffed. "You drove all the way down here to talk to me," he said. "Why?" He had one hand on the steering wheel and one hand on his thigh. "There were other writers that came to talk to me," he said. "People that wanted to know about me and my guys. But I didn't like them."

A long finger pointed to my head. "You'll do."

At the time I thought he was just surprised that anyone cared. He'd been trying to get people to care for a long time.

"By the way," he said, "you religious?"

I hesitated long enough for him to fill his mouth with a fresh wad of chew. I didn't want the conversation to come down to this. Finally I told him I wasn't.

"Good," he said.

He sat quietly, just blinking, but everything inside him seemed to churn.

In Dalton, Caleb stopped the truck and disappeared into a building that looked coughed up by the earth. He returned engineless. "Wrong store," he said, and slipped into the truck.

"So I don't read the Bible that good," he said. We turned onto a dirt road. "But there's a hierarchy of angels, you know that, right? They have ranks just like the military has ranks. It's hard to tell the difference at first between angels and demons, but over time you learn."

"I thought you weren't religious."

"Spiritual," he said. "There's a difference." Caleb sucked his lips under his teeth. "I hate religion. I think religious people are worse than people who hate God. Religious means, 'I read my Bible and I go to church every Sunday and I do this and I do that and the good Lord does this.' You see. They believe in God but only because their daddy told them to believe."

He started to move around in his seat as if there were a weasel in his pants.

"What's happening," I said.

"Hang on," he said. Caleb stuck his hand out the window. "I'm getting something." His eyeballs rolled and he sat straight-backed like an antenna picking up waves from somewhere far away.

"What is it? What's going on?"

"I don't know," he said. "Wasn't real clear." He twitched like a fly-bothered horse. "Sometimes I'll be walking down the street and I'll have to stop. A text message from God kinda thing."

"Intuition," I said.

"Call it whatever you want."

I wrote *sees future* in my notebook.

I asked if he knew any other veterans that were seeing their dead buddies. "My friend Valarie," he said. "She makes dinner for her dead husband every night." He whistled and tapped the steering wheel. "But you might have some trouble getting her to talk about it. A lot of guys have a hard time talking about it. They see PTSD, like you say, as when you go back and you experience those memories. I'd say for the majority of guys, they can't figure out what it is." He scratched his sideburns and cracked his neck by taking both hands off the wheel.

We drove on until the land turned from vine-gnarled to barren, and towns bloomed with a stark suddenness into neon strip malls and restaurants with names like Chin Chin China, and a Hummer dealership where a purple ape balloon waved its hand below an American flag so heavy it could hardly lift itself.

"Think about a girl that gets raped," he said. "It's the day-to-day things that start it back up for the raped girl. Like someone holding her wrist, and that's when the emotions rise up. But see out there, it's so big and so traumatic that you don't even have time to deal with it, you can't process it, your brain can't process it." He spread his arms wide and his knuckles clacked the windshield. "The world is just kinda shit for about twenty minutes and then it's over. It's mostly just reacting and then you think about it years later when you're home."

He kept glancing at me with large, almond-shaped eyes that blinked heavily as if always in a state of waking. They were canine blue and rimmed with black lashes. "In the beginning," he said, "I refused to believe I had a handicap—that it was PTSD. I didn't want it to be PTSD. PTSD means you're an outcast. It means you're the crazy one. I probably had PTSD, but there's always the influence of the demonic."

Then I knew that God was just a word he used to talk about other things.

"It's something that a lot of people aren't going to want to hear about. Some people aren't going to believe it at all. But I think it will change how they understand PTSD."

He took me to Mi Casa, a Mexican restaurant across from a strip mall outside Atlanta, and we ate cheese enchiladas and drank Coke from plastic cups brought to us by a pretty girl with a bee-stung face. We sat at a booth away from the door.

Caleb told me a story about his ex-wife, Allyson. "While I was deployed," he said, "the dog got pregnant and miscarried. The miscarried puppies were in a pile on the floor and Allyson had to call me in Iraq to ask what to do. I told her to put the dead dogs in the trash, but she wouldn't do it. When I got home, the dead dogs were still in the house."

He took his fork to his plate. He covered his mouth to swallow.

"That's the kind of shit I had to come home to," he said.

Not the first time I wondered whether Caleb was remembering what the war made him see.

When I asked Caleb about his missions, he formed his Copenhagen snuff into a fine ball and told me he didn't want to talk about Special Forces or ragheads or Saddam. He didn't want to talk about his buddy who got his skull blown off and how he had to duct-tape it back on, "brains and all." Or about Fluffy, that cat he peeled and ate dead off the side of the road, "still soft and cat-looking." He didn't want to talk about mistaking water balloons for grenades or those women with AKs. He wanted to talk about the day his entire unit died, how he thought he heard their falling, burning voices from a desk in an empty room at headquarters. He wanted to talk about how his ex-wife called him a murderer and then made him take out the trash. He wanted to talk about his friend Valarie who made dinner for her dead husband every night. He wanted to talk about how all of it was still there, every day, the blood in his mouth, the screaming, his dead buddies. He wanted to talk about after the war.

"When I got home three years ago," Caleb said, "I'd have this thing come visit me in the middle of the night. You could hear it coming down the hallway." He stood up in the booth, hunched his shoulders, and started walking apishly in place. Boom, he said, slapping the table. *Boom*. A few customers turned their heads.

"This thing," he told me, "a big dark figure, opened my door. It was so tall it had to lean down to get its head through. In this really deep voice it said, *I will kill you if you proceed.* It sounded almost like it wanted an answer back from me, and so I started laughing at it and I said, 'You've got to be face-fucking me.'"

The customer across from us got up to leave. Caleb finished his Coke and spit his chew into the empty cup.

"But it came back every night. One time I'm sitting in my room and it walks in, shuts the door, and comes after me. It starts to choke me. I'm physically choking. My dead buddy Kip comes in and wrestles it off me. But Kip isn't stronger than this thing either so it chokes him too. Kip was taking the punishment for me. I'm watching this and I'm freaking out."

"Punishment for what?" I asked.

"For killing," he said, "and for living."

The air conditioner groaned and strings of dust swirled in the rushed, grated air. Caleb turned sideways, leaned his back against the wall, and rested his legs on the booth.

I asked if he'd ever gone to the VA for help and he said he waited in line for two days and came home chewing painkillers.

"A hundred and forty vets are dead every week because of shit like this. The VA doesn't do anything. I'm pushing the verge of crazy to save these guys." He put a napkin to his mouth, and his hands folded into its curves. The white looked clean against his skin. "I was one of the best-trained soldiers in the army. They spent millions training me how to go to war, but they never taught me how to come home."

I dug an article out of my purse that I'd been carrying around about the twenty-six-year-old soldier named Sergeant Brian Rand who shot himself after being followed night after night by the ghost of the Iraqi man he'd killed. I'd talked to his sister April on the phone and intended to drive to North Carolina for an interview after I spoke to Caleb.

Brian had been stationed at a Fallujah checkpoint with his buddy Chris. The guys were bored. Not much had happened that day until a white van started coming up the road toward them, picking up speed. Brian turned to Chris and asked him what he thought they should do. Chris replied, "Shoot him, I guess." Brian shot him.

The dead Iraqi man came to North Carolina and choked Brian while he slept and demanded an apology for the killing.

He told April. She said do whatever the Iraqi man said to do. Brian apologized but the dead man wouldn't listen. Join me on the other side, the man said.

Caleb read the article slowly, scrunched it into a ball, and threw it at me.

"This is the same thing that visited me." He pointed his finger at it. "Everything," he said. "From how it's talking to him. To how his friends think he's talking to himself. To how he thinks he needs to die. I've heard the story thousands of times. It's no different than mine. A lot of guys I've worked with, you would never get this out of them. Never. You talk about this and you'll lose your career. You'll never go back to combat. You're the crazy guy. Your wife won't believe you."

"You don't think hallucinations are a part of PTSD?" I asked.

Caleb switched the chew from one side of his mouth to the other. He looked to the side, waved to the waitress.

"I know this is gonna sound crazy to you," he said, leaning forward, getting close to my face, "but this isn't PTSD."

The room was full of the smell of grease, the sound of air-conditioning. I watched him chew, the way his jaw muscles flexed to the size of walnuts. He wiped sauce from his teeth.

"This thing," he said, "this big, black thing—it can come after anyone. It can come after you and kill you and it will try to destroy you. It's no joke."

The Black Thing.

He said it does not represent anything and that it's like nothing we know here in this world. He said it's not a metaphor because there are no metaphors for this kind of evil. It was shadow. It was death. It was the gathered souls of all his dead friends.

"Do you know when it's coming?" I said.

He put his hands out on either side of him, palms flat as if he were trapped inside a box. "I'll be in a room just like this one," he said, "and all at once the windows will go dark. And then the Black Thing just sort of seeps in."

When Caleb returned to Georgia in 2005, he started seeing the chopper's tail number—#146—everywhere. He went out for Mexican and received $1.46 in change. This was his last bit of cash. So he figured he might as well try for a Lotto ticket. Its number: 146, bought at 1:46 in the afternoon. He won five hundred bucks. At night he woke to see the clock flash 1:46.

Caleb and Krissy ended their relationship. She couldn't take all the waking up at night, all the talking to Kip and the Black Thing, or the way they wrestled.

Caleb didn't own much, a few suitcases and a toolbox. He carried a piece of the blown-up chopper with him, salvaged from the Hindu Kush. A black rectangle, printed with the words *Evil Empire* in white letters. He'd kept it in the garage.

An old friend, an army guy named Ryan living near Atlanta, rented a room to Caleb for cheap. They'd known each other since seventh grade.

Ryan deployed to Iraq and Caleb stayed home. Aimless and unemployed and consumed by memories of the dead soldiers, most days he spent on the couch, watching television and drinking beer with Ryan's stepfather, a Lakota Indian named Wombly.

Wombly was a big guy with loose black hair that fanned his breasts. One day Wombly raised his beer in the air and said, "Who's that dead guy that keeps following you around?"

It was the first time anybody had seen Kip. Caleb thought Kip was just PTSD. "You see him too?" Caleb said.

Wombly sucked beer from the rim of his can. The ghosts annoyed him, floating around the television. "And who's that handsome boy?"

He described Major Reich's blue eyes, the wedding ring. Al Gore's mustache. Sergeant First Class Muralles. Master Sergeant Tre Ponder. All of them.

Wombly invited Caleb to a sweat lodge in the woods. There were other Indians there and they all sat naked together in the steam, seeing spirits and getting visions. Caleb saw dead soldiers in the smoke. He saw old Indian warriors. The buffalo god Tatanka.

Wombly believed Caleb had special powers and offered to train him to become a medicine man.

Caleb agreed. His skin took on the smell of cedar plank and wood smoke. He stayed for months, memorized the names of healing plants: wormwood, horsemint, skunk cabbage. The names of gods: Gnas and Han and Etu.

Men and women visited Wombly at the sweat lodge, pleading for help. A lady came with arthritis in her legs and Caleb watched one of Wombly's friends pray over her, and as he prayed, the arthritis went into him, into his fingers, and his fingers twisted like gnarled wood. He had to get them amputated. Wombly trained Caleb about ancient cures, lost spirits, and displaced souls. He taught Caleb how to bridge the human and the spiritual realms.

When Caleb finished training he thought he'd found a way to control the Black Thing. For two weeks, he thought it was gone.

But it returned. Caleb remembered what Wombly taught him. He said stop and it stopped. Caleb said be still and it was still. Caleb said now stop choking Kip and it stopped choking Kip.

When he told the story, he said he told the Black Thing, "You expect me to fear you? Do you have any idea what I have been through in my life? Your big black ass does not offend me coming here, in my house. You're not going to scare me. Get the fuck out of my house." And it left.

Around this time Caleb started getting his hair cut at a one-room barbershop in Kennesaw from a Baptist named Sophie. She was the kind of hairdresser who talked while Caleb listened. Sophie told Caleb about how a tree branch ripped right through her bedroom window. Caleb offered up his own room. Told Sophie he'd stay in a hotel. She moved in right away. Caleb would be there during the day, usually in the garage, fixing up the car on a rolling board near the cement where it was cool. One of these days Sophie came up to him while he was lying on his back covered in oil. "If you just want to fool around sometime and have sex," she said, "we can. No strings attached." Caleb said it doesn't work that way but they had sex anyway and then they started dating.

One night, with arms wrapped around Sophie's small frame, Caleb woke. The moon was near his window. Its light spilled across the floor like a veil. Sophie's long black hair looked like an oily slick on which her head floated. She put her feet together so that one foot rested in the arch of the other and her hands clasped as if in prayer beneath her chin.

The Black Thing said *I will kill you if you proceed.*

Then Caleb just started laughing. He told the Black Thing— whatever it was, he still didn't know if it was in his head, or if it was real, or if he was going crazy—he said, "No you won't, asshole, because I'm going to do it myself." He grabbed his 9mm, loaded it up. "I'm done," he said. "I'm checking out. I don't fit in this world."

He was back on the tarmac hearing Kip's promise of death.

Caleb told God he couldn't take it anymore. "I've hung in. I've done everything I've known to do." He got his gun and drove to a hotel. He pressed the muzzle to his temple. "Now, God, if you're there and I have a purpose in my life, by the count of three, you better stop me. If you're that powerful, then you better give me a reason to be alive. You better stop me."

Caleb started counting.

One.

"If you're that powerful, God, then you better give me a reason to be alive. You better stop me."

Two.

And on *two* the phone rang. It was 1:46 in the morning. On the line was his fishing buddy Marshall. His wife was going into labor and he needed Caleb's help.

He drove to the hospital. His saliva still tasted like metal when the baby came.

• • •

It wasn't easy to disentangle from his relationship with Sophie. She was still hanging around the house, eating from his fridge. She still had her bags in his living room. She had become friends with his roommate, Ryan. One evening, Caleb thought he heard Ryan giving Sophie a hot oil massage on his bed. He waited outside the doorway, listening. "Caleb will break pretty soon," Ryan said. "I've been sending stuff to him in the middle of the night. I've been sending the scariest of all scary things into Caleb's room in the middle of the night."

It was the voice of the Black Thing.

Everywhere Caleb went he heard its voice. One time, he was in the kitchen, thinking about lunch. Ryan was sitting on the couch. "Tacos or burritos?" Caleb asked.

Fuck you, Ryan said, *this is war.*

"Ryan, what the fuck are you talking about?"

"Dude, I want tacos."

It happened over and over again. *In the end you aren't going to win,* said the voice coming out of Ryan.

So a year had passed. Caleb was still seeing Kip. He was still seeing the Black Thing. Smoke curled through his windows at night. The air smelled like burned flesh. Then, tired of everything, he drove to the Allatoona reservoir, where he'd been spending days fixing up an old canoe. It was the only thing he seemed able to fix. Allatoona had emerald water that deepened in the summer. He pushed the canoe out, jumped inside, and paddled to the lake's center. He thought about how he should have been on that chopper. He thought about sinking coldly into the lake, letting his lungs starve. Rain filled the canoe and absorbed into his socks. "All right, God," he said. "I'll try anything at this point because I'm about to kill myself." It was about three in the morning. He got out his gun. If he pulled the trigger, the bullet would take his body and set it on the canoe's side. Blood would spill into Allatoona. "I was built to serve men and right now I have nobody to serve because everybody is dead. I can't even serve my own children because they're gone. You give me a reason to live and I will do whatever you want me to do. I'm a soldier and I need a mission." The rain stopped and showed him the moon. Its light tore and scattered the water. There were voices in the dark. He thought he heard Kip speaking to him, all of them, his dead friends, murmuring in the leaves.

Caleb paddled swiftly back to shore, his clothes heavy and wet. He crawled through the mud on all fours like something just born from the lake, back to his room, into his sheets, into bed.

At Mi Casa, when I mentioned to Caleb that I would be visiting Sergeant Brian Rand's sister April Somdahl in North Carolina, he asked to see the article about the dead Iraqi man. I handed it to him and his fingers traced the sentences.

"You shouldn't go," he said. "It's blatantly a Destroyer demon. Blatantly." It had a name.

"It's from Afghanistan?"

"Afghanistan made it bigger. A Destroyer is a destroyer. It pretty much destroys everything. If this woman has a Destroyer on her, which I know she does, then it's going to come after you."

I must have looked skeptical because he raised his arms above his head to help me imagine it. He had an animal sheen in his eyes that made him look sad, not ravenous in the way he might have wanted right then.

He explained how he came to know the demons. Another veteran brought him to meet a minister and his wife in the town of Portal, Georgia, where the layer between heaven and earth is very thin, and they removed a demon from Caleb. That was that. The Destroyer, the war demon. The minister called it deliverance.

"What are you doing carrying around that article?" he asked. "Let me tell you. You're finding patterns. Now you need to figure how to tell your story. Are you going to tell people that there's this big old demon that runs around and controls people and makes them flip out and makes them kill themselves?"

I asked if he saw the demons in the same way he saw me sitting there in front of him. Or was it just a sense?

"I see them," he said. "I see them every day. But you get used to it. It's like if five guys walked in here with guns on their hips, would you feel awkward?"

I told him I would.

"Well, I wouldn't because everyone in combat has guns on their hips. It's the same thing with demons. Yeah, there's this big scary beast sitting next to you and you're just like *hi*. It can't really bother you."

Caleb said he wanted to teach me something he used to do in the military. He reached his hands across the table. He wanted to practice the sixth sense. "Everyone operates in that state to a degree. It's not abnormal." He called to me with his fingers. "Hold them," he said. "Hold them and look at me." I wasn't sure what to make of his stories yet, so I just followed his lead. I took his hands into mine, bony and warm. We stared at each other without blinking and then he told me to shut my eyes. I watched. "Shut your eyes," he cooed, as if he knew. But when I shut them he was still there, a dark figure on the inside of my eyelids.

He unleashed his grip, and his eyes fluttered and he scribbled on a notepad with his tongue out, eager as a schoolboy.

"Okay," he said. "What'd you get?"

"I didn't get anything."

He put his elbows on the table, and his eyebrows touched. "I got *warrior*," he said. "You're a warrior and you're on a mission."

Caleb's muscles tightened. He stared past me. "You ever feel the air go cold in the room? A hand on your shoulder? The hair on the back of your neck stand on end?" He said there was something in the room. He stared slack-jawed behind me. I craned my neck to look. When I returned to his face he seemed to smile in this small victory. "You're going to need something bigger than what you've got," he said. "Angels will show themselves in the form of what they do. Same as demons."

"What do you think I have?" I said. I wanted to know his intentions. He started pacing.

"I'm going to tell you a lot of things that you might not like," Caleb said. "I'll throw some words out there—some of them sound like Bible words: good and evil, light and dark. As you talk to these soldiers, what you're doing is shining a light on the issue, saying here is this big, ugly thing. Then they're going to get pissed off and come after you. You can fight them. But not if it's bigger than what you're walking around with. Then it's going to make your life a living hell."

Caleb pressed his finger to his skull and started to think. He kept tapping his head as if his finger were a magnet and whatever he wanted to say would rise out of him. He seemed to still be figuring out what to tell me.

"You have your dead grandma," he said. "Now. Let's say this gal April in North Carolina were to have a Destroyer on her. The Destroyer has more rank in the angelic realm than April. What would you do in that situation to fight this thing? How would you combat this thing?"

I said nothing.

"These things can jump on to things that don't have authority over them. If you don't have protection they can jump right on to you too. If they're bigger than the army you're walking around with, it's going to make your life a living hell. It's tough. You don't have authority by yourself. You only have authority with the army. Deliverance is like entrance into the army."

"So if I get this army then I can observe a deliverance session?"

"You have to receive deliverance to get the army." His eyes travel over me in a slippery way. "Like I said, you're going to need some bigger guns than you have."

"How do you know if you've been demonized?"

"You don't know. You'll probably never know. Unless you're Jesus Christ or have been through deliverance you're probably going to have a demon on you. Might not be as bad as the next guy. It will give you protection—an army—against this thing when it comes after you. Call it PTSD. Call it demons, call it whatever you want, but if that gal has a Destroyer on her, it's going to come after you. I guarantee it."

He recommended I talk to the minister in Portal. "Stick around, Georgia," he said. "And you'll witness."

His mouth was as thin and dark as a line of pencil. "This whole demon thing. It's just like the military. The demons don't have a high ranking. Unless you're in the kingdom of darkness thinking." He got up, went to the bathroom, and came back.

I asked if he ever knew anyone he killed. I asked him all those questions you're not supposed to ask, about killing, and how many you killed, and death and destruction, and I asked him about morals.

"Was the war moral? Was that a woman, or was that a kid? Did you kill people? I'm tired of all these questions. There's no moral or immoral. All that shit goes out the window. You don't even think about it. You make a decision so fast it's like a car crash. After 9/11 everyone wanted us to hunt these guys down. But then, when we're out there in the blood and guts, pulling the trigger, everyone's like: *you're immoral.* The world is different over there. Women and kids pull guns on you and try to kill you. Five- and six-year-olds running around out there with AKs."

Caleb jiggled his Coke. "You usually can tell if someone's pulled the trigger. Go to a bar and find the biggest shit-talker, the one saying, 'I can't wait to pull the trigger' or 'I mowed down those dudes' or 'I killed them.' Those are the guys that have never climaxed, but once they get to climax, they'll never brag about it. They'll never do it. Never. But I've seen people that are very antikilling anybody yank that trigger and hose people down because it came to them or theirs. Would I do it again if I had to? Yeah. Would I walk around and drink a couple beers and try to fight somebody? No. I won't fight somebody to take their girlfriend home. If I'm going to fight someone, I'm going to fight to kill. People have some issues with the whole contracted killer thing. I don't have a problem with it. I may have just been there too long," he added. "I don't know."

A few motorcyclists cramped a nearby booth. They used tortilla chips to sponge spilled beer. One of their women did a stripper dance with her eyes closed.

"Now," he said, "losing your virginity is a good metaphor for killing."

He'd lost it to a girl named Tamika. He took off his clothes and asked, what do I do? And Tamika took off her clothes and leaned against the bed with her hands pressed against the mattress. And then, again, he said, what do I do? And she showed him what to do in the way a mother might show her child how to fold a napkin. When it was over Caleb went to the railroad tracks and watched a tangerine sunrise and thought, *big fucking deal*.

"Big fucking deal," he said about killing.

He stood up. He was like a bird making his feathers known. "Imagine," he said, and then he sat down again and tucked his hands away from me. "Imagine that you're in a room and it's just you and this friend and the room is full of big guys. These big guys corner you. One of the big guys says, *Who is going to get raped?* Here's the deal. You're not a virgin. She is. You have to choose who gets raped." He slopped a triangle of quesadilla in his mouth. "Who gets raped?"

He put a plug of tobacco in his cheek, pressed it deep with his thumb.

"I get raped," I said. And he nodded as if this were evidence of my decency. "Once you experience the death and destruction, it's the same kind of feeling."

The waitress refilled his Coke. The virginity metaphor continued.

"Think about it this way. When you make out and you almost get to climax without any repercussions, well, then, climax is like this dangling carrot. It's something you want to experience. So many climaxes. So much getting ready. There comes a point when the carrot looks tastier than waiting on the carrot. Eventually you'll cross the barrier, and when you cross that barrier, it's not what you expected it to be. So now that you've had sex, you don't go around talking about it as much."

He reminded me of the day he stepped off the *Evil Empire* and picked the severed fingers out of the tie-down rings, like a cold-blooded American killer, he said. "I know those maintenance guys are still swapping scary stories about me. All bloody and crazy." But Caleb saw it differently. "I was sitting there in tears, all alone, by myself, washing blood out of the aircraft, praying none of those guys had to see what I just saw."

He sucked ice out of his Coke and let it melt and crack between his teeth. "What happened to the fingers?"

"I gave the fingers to the medics," he said. "They tried to put them back on."

Caleb had an appointment to meet a man he called colonel at a military vehicle factory near Carthage, North Carolina, not far from the place where he completed SERE school at Camp Mackall. He needed to pick up two vehicles for his company. The colonel would give them to Caleb at no cost. He invited me along.

Caleb said he couldn't tell me the name of the factory, but when we arrived the name was on a sign outside the building.

It took us two days. We made the drive with Buck, the broker from Kennesaw. Buck was bald and turned red when he spoke. A few years ago, Buck jumped out of a plane, landed wrong, legs straight instead of bent, and bones broke, femur to skull. "My wife had to wipe my ass for six months after the fall," he said. He thanked her for this openly and in a serious manner at a barbecue that was also a religious gathering. He ran his fingers over the place where his spine humped.

On the drive, Caleb only listened to country and Buck to rap. Buck kept switching the Johnny Cash to Tupac. Buck only drank Mountain Dew, and Caleb drank Coke. They spoke with hand gestures and spit their words. We drove late into the night. Caleb said he didn't need to sleep, ever really. We passed a wide lake torn by the long arms of swamp plants.

"Everyone knows about the war," Buck said. "You should just go home. We all already know too much about the war."

Buck started swearing at me, and telling Caleb to stop bringing God into the workings of things. Slurping. Shifting. Buck turned his face back at me, as far as his neck would twist without his body moving. Words came from the side of his mouth.

At two in the morning we stopped at a roadside motel with no hallways. The bedroom windows faced a parking lot. Our rooms shared a wall. In my pillow I heard Caleb and Buck fight over the bed. Buck lost. Thumb-sized cockroaches cleaned their wings. Caleb said to be up early but they didn't wake until noon. They knocked on my door and I responded through the wood, met them later in the breakfast room, overlooking a leaf-clotted pool. The room had blue carpet, fake Monet paintings, cornflakes, and old ladies on a field trip. The corner television played disaster footage of a flood somewhere far away.

"What's the grossest thing you ever ate?" Buck said.

"Dead cat," said Caleb. "We ate bugs and other stuff. Mealworms would squirt in your mouth. Stole a chicken from a farm. I fucking hate chickens. Chickens are dinosaurs with shrunken heads."

The vehicle factory was in the woods, big as two football fields, full of jeeps with heavy machinery, gun racks, missile launchers. A room marked Top Secret. Greased mechanics with masks stood behind flamed rods. Caleb negotiated with the colonel, who paced with his arms wide and his shoulders square and he had a pair of brows thick and gray as storm clouds. When he spoke he tugged on the belt of his too-high pants, lifting them enough to show high-top sneakers and white socks. Caleb disappeared into an office with Buck and the colonel. He said I couldn't go in there. I waited in the front seat of a machine-gun-mounted jeep and fell asleep until a shirtless, freckled man, six feet tall and covered in coarse, red hair pushed my shoulder. He had on overalls with an unclasped strap.

"I'm Red," he said in an accent that sounded like a wobbling saw. Sweat stood on his skin. He gave me his hand and I took it. "Caleb said to entertain you." He pointed toward the office where Caleb spoke to the colonel. "He said take her in the growler."

They were light utility vehicles with Kevlar seats. This particular growler had eight wheels and looked like a toy race car with an open top and no doors. One seat belt went over the head and strapped across the chest to be buckled on either side of the body. A separate seat belt covered the legs.

"Want to go for a ride?" he said.

Caleb stepped out of the office, grinning. "Have fun," he said. We drove off a washboard ramp and made a hard right onto a country highway. "Yes, ma'am, give me anything with wheels and I'm gravy," he said. The seats vibrated and Red whistled. He touched his beard.

We cut down a dirt road and Red stopped the vehicle. It jerked. I put my hand on my seat belt latch. "Racehorse got running today," he said, stepping out of the vehicle and into the woods. He unzipped his pants and pissed roadside. A wide puddle spread on the red clay earth. He shook his hips. A beetle cooled itself in the pee foam.

At a nearby town Red went searching for machine parts. The town was a collection of one-story metal buildings with essential purposes: gas, food, truck.

Red bought lug nuts. I waited in the growler. The wind dragged a paper bag across the cement. Six men came out of the store. Old men with urine-colored beards. The tallest man chewed something. One of them had a fake leg or else a leg so emaciated that when the wind blew, the fabric hugged the width of bone.

"Where'd you get that car?" he asked. "Woman shouldn't be in a car like that," he said.

"Not all alone she shouldn't," the tall man said.

The colonel agreed to give Caleb two growlers at no cost. Caleb agreed to bring in enough profits later to pay him off. We sat at foldout tables at a diner in Carthage called the Village Place. Everyone was ex-military and everyone ordered the Club Deluxe on white bread with mayonnaise served in aluminum packets. The waitresses were cigarette-voiced, young, pregnant, and kind.

The men talked about submarines and World War II and how it's better to pilot planes than submarines because at least in a plane you know you'll come back to the ground.

One of the factory workers told Caleb about an idea he had for a vehicle called Brute.

Caleb's eyes widened and he moved around in his seat.

The Brute can float and swim. She's not pretty to look at. She was designed to service oil rigs. Rescue the stranded. Explore uninhabited lands.

Caleb had mentioned the name to me on the drive, and so I asked, "Wasn't Brute your idea." Caleb raised his index finger to his mouth, indicating that I ought to hush. He said don't talk about the visions.

The colonel stood to use the restroom. Caleb leaned in. "Red wants to work for me."

"And?"

"I hate redheads," he said. "Can't trust them."

"What if I showed up as a redhead?"

"I knew you weren't just by talking to you on the phone."

In the back of the restaurant a man put soap on the metal hook where his hand should have been.

The clouds moved in great white herds. Caleb stacked the vehicles on a multicar trailer hitched to the pickup. In Georgia somewhere we pulled off the highway and parked in a wide dirt area the shape of a horseshoe. Some kids were drinking in their jeep, boys in the front, girls in the back, the trunk a glittery pile of smashed cans. They cheered when they saw the growlers, and then started their engine and sank into the woods. We parked in front of the steep dirt slope that rose almost vertically before it flattened and connected to the area where the kids had just been. Buck pulled out a video camera. Caleb jumped in one of the growlers and crawled up a steep rise of dirt. The growler lurched. Something inside broke. We watched it roll slowly back down the hill. Caleb took his shirt off and swore. "You didn't just see that," he said. Caleb sent Buck away to buy the broken parts.

Caleb looked huge. There were clouds all around him. We sat in the growler and stayed quiet for some time.

"So you want an example of the Destroyer?" Caleb said. Do you remember the conversation with Buck in the truck?"

"Which one? We were in the truck for nine hours."

"The one where he was getting all testy. Do you remember when

I cut it off? When Buck was saying, 'This is what you should do and this is what I think.' Remember? That was the Destroyer talking."

"You're suggesting that the Destroyer was inhabiting Buck?"

"It wasn't inhabiting him," he said. "It was working through him. He lives with it every day. It's almost funny because sometimes it's so overplayed that you're just like, Okay. Gotcha. I see your ugly head."

He'd reminded me about DeeAnne and the boat engine she wanted. The one he was looking for the first day we met. "When I told her I couldn't find the boat engine she called me a son of a bitch to my face. She told me to burn in hell. She said, Caleb, you're a failure and you're a waste. But you've got to understand that this lady is just some lady with a broke-down boat. She can call me a son of a bitch to my face as many times as she wants and I'm not mad at her. I don't think she's the problem. It's the other guy at the negotiation table who's the problem."

Caleb picked a gnat out of his eye, wet and dead.

"Essentially what came out was this big nasty thing." He made his hands like claws and stretched them apart. "But in the truck the other night with Buck, it was very sly: *Here, bite this.*"

An hour passed. Buck returned with no car parts, just cheeseburgers from Wendy's. We ate the cheeseburgers in the growler, in its shade. No one spoke. The heat was getting to Buck. He shone like a glass ball. Finally he walked away from us and stood silently in the sun with Caleb's shirt over his head. He looked like someone waiting for an execution but who, in the end, was too unimportant to kill.

Caleb and his wife, Eden, lived in a two-story house near Woodstock, Georgia, not far from Wombly's sweat lodge. There were acres between homes. Cardboard signs advertising eggs. A few horses twitched from green, large-bodied flies.

The only light was from the dusk—a soft blue. The house was quiet and the air-conditioning cold. Moths hit the windows, and in the basement a dryer hummed. Caleb sat at a long oak table across from Eden. She was the daughter of the minister who brought Caleb through deliverance. He married her after the exorcism. She was twenty-five, taught kindergarten. Robust in the hips with translucent skin, pale as if descended from Vikings. She had blond hair but dyed it blonder.

Isabel and Isaac, his children from Allyson, sat between them. He'd lost custody after the divorce. He saw them only a few weeks a year. Isabel wore a Barbie nightshirt, and Isaac, faded sleep pants but no shirt. Isaac looked just like his father. He was five years old but there was very little baby left in him. He looked tan, muscled, and mean.

The kids gripped forks over empty plates, and Eden stood up to pull a pizza out of the oven, wearing pink running shorts, walking barefoot. Caleb waited at the head of the table, looking ordinary.

"Would you like some pizza?" Eden said. She took off one oven mitt and ran a hand through her hair, soft like running water.

Caleb pointed at the living room wall with a fork.

"The walls," he said, "they look blue, don't they?" He wiped his mouth with his hand.

"But they're purple. It has to do with the light. I'm actually good at home decorating."

"Do you want something to drink?" Eden asked. "We have Kool-Aid."

"Kool-Aid is great," I said.

We all sat down at the table, drinking Kool-Aid. I asked how she and Caleb met.

"How did we meet?" Eden said, looking off to the side, biting her lip. She rested her chin in her hand, touched her pizza with her fork, and then put her fork down.

"She knows my story," Caleb said. "Tell her yours."

"Well, he was over at my parents' house," Eden said, "getting delivered, and when I saw him standing there talking to my dad, he gave me a look like this." Eden widened her eyes, cocked her head. "He did that with these really big crazy eyes. And I thought, *oh, this guy is weird.* I shook his hand or whatever and then just went in the other room and played on the computer."

She kept her eyes on Caleb but her head turned toward me. "Go on," he said. "It's okay."

"The next day," Eden said, "we had a bonfire and a cookout, and we were shooting guns. My girlfriends were over and they wanted me to go talk to him. I think he's thirty-five, I said. And see, I was twenty-five and that would just be gross to date someone that old. Then one girl said, I think he's only twenty-six. And then another came over and said, yeah, just checked, he's twenty-six. So I decided to go over there and teach him how to shoot guns because he wasn't shooting very good."

Caleb said nothing. He had his hands folded.

"Then later Caleb told me I was his wife. He said, *you are my wife.* You know, you don't just say that to somebody. I mean," she added, "men have been using God as an excuse to date me for so long. You know, being a pastor's kid, men are always saying they were sent by God."

Isaac dropped his pizza on the table. He grabbed the pizza and pushed it into his mouth, cheese side down.

"But I knew she was my wife," Caleb said. "I'd seen her before. Then I'm thinking, oh, no, that's this guy's daughter—that's the minister's daughter. How do I tell him? I went back to work and I was sitting there at that dealership and we weren't making any money. I thought, you know what? My wife is down there and I don't know what I am going to do for work but if I know anything, I know that that is my wife down there. So I moved to Portal. I called her brother and told him but I didn't tell anyone why I moved because I knew they'd think I was crazy."

Eden took over the story. "Caleb came back to Portal and he didn't have a place to live and he was hanging around the house during the day, staying in a hotel at night. 'Are you doing ministry with my parents?' He said no and walked away. I didn't really get an answer from him. He looked like he needed some help so I decided I'd help him look for a place to rent. I drove him around town and we ended up in the Walmart parking lot until three in the morning. You know that country radio song about being in the Walmart parking lot?" Eden asked.

"Never heard of it," I said.

"It's great. I'll get you a copy. Anyway, it turns out he'd been in Atlanta for a while, praying for a wife."

"I was done with dating people," Caleb said, "and done with not being married. I was aiming to get a wife."

"Caleb had three dreams," Eden said, "one about me as a kid, one about me in my forties, and one about me as an old woman with long gray hair. A month before he came, I was sleeping in my room and I saw something flying around the ceiling. I never saw anything. I'm not a seer. I ran into my parents' room, screaming, and they got rid of it. Two weeks before I met him I saw it again, flying around the room. All of a sudden I saw this man's face just looking at me. It was a man's face," she said. "And it was *his* face."

"I saw the same thing flying around my room," Caleb said. "Only it was *her* face."

"But I was so closed off with my heart and my mind because I would be getting married to this other guy with a crazy family. He was really strong and controlling. He was verbally abusive."

"Don't ask about him," Caleb said. "He doesn't matter."

Eden said she had to pray hard about whether Caleb was her husband. She prayed. Nobody else knew that she was praying. She prayed that everybody in her family—all nine people—needed to hear something from God, on their own. Everybody in her whole family never liked anyone she ever dated, that's why she asked. Turns out her father had heard already. He was in the bathroom washing his hands when he looked up and heard the Lord's voice say, *That is Eden's husband.*

Caleb pointed at his chest.

"When my mom was vacuuming, she heard the Lord say, *He will love her more than life itself.*"

Her sisters had dreams.

"My brother heard from God when we were out shooting. I was shooting his gun, it was huge, and he was standing behind me. He had his left hand on my shoulder, and his right hand out in case I dropped it. I was kneeling down and aiming. It was gonna give me a big kick. The Lord said, *Caleb will guide her and protect her.* Another lady that we are kinda friends with had something else too.

"Honey," she said, interrupting herself, "can you pass me another piece of pizza?"

"Then turns out we both wrote lists," Caleb said. "Eden wrote hers when she was sixteen. One hundred and ten things she wanted in a man. I had my own list. Guess what? They were exactly the same."

It didn't take long. Eden canceled her marriage to a man she didn't love and started a new one with Caleb. They had the ceremony in June 2007. Caleb wore a white tux and the minister walked his daughter up the aisle.

After dinner Caleb shuffled to the freezer. It made a growling sound. He disappeared into its cold light, returned with Popsicles. "Thai Thai," he said. "Isabel Goose," he said. The children ran to him. He kneeled.

"When God speaks," I said, "what does that sound like to you?"

"When God speaks," she said, "it's a very strong inner thought.

People are lying if they say they hear God's voice because it's not a voice. It's a consciousness."

"It plays like a video," Caleb said, putting his elbows on the table.

"I don't get those," Eden said. "Sometimes it's just knowledge. Everyone has different styles. Even when it's crazy like what Caleb saw in the army."

"Remember how I told you there's going to be a flood in July?" Caleb said. He'd had a few prophecies for me. One included a flood in July and another that I'd marry a dirty farm boy. "Well, when this stuff comes down the pipe people will say, oh, how'd you know that? Because the day before you were crazy."

"But you *are* crazy, honey," Eden said, rubbing his back. "The Lord is actually talking all the time. It's like a radio station. You have to tune your ear into it. I don't know why, but I'm a little slower than others. I'm trying to figure out how to trust my own instinct. Once you start to get it, he will talk to you more and more and you will start to see crazy things. My sister, she has the gift of seeing, just like my dad."

"It's like how we trained in Special Ops. The sixth sense. It works both ways. The dark side has the same giftings. I view it as a war, as a battle going on out there. You are either fighting on one side or the other."

"What if you don't hear anything?" I said.

"If you don't hear anything," he said, "then you aren't on either side."

Before he met Eden, Caleb's time with Wombly gave him head-space enough to hire eight men from flyers stapled to telephone poles. He started a construction company that served rich people in the Atlanta suburb of Buckhead, fixing unnecessary technology like voice-automated torchlights for driveways, refrigerated wine cellars with video security. He was running a profit until one of the workers stole all the money and ran away. It wasn't much, but it was everything. He worked three months with no pay so that he could give paychecks to the rest of his men.

Once again, he'd lost everything.

Caleb quit the construction job and started work at Canton Chevrolet. Quit that too. Started work at Meineke. The cement there was always cool and he liked the way it felt on his skin when he pressed his hands on the ground to lower himself beneath a truck. He knew the inside of a truck as he knew a body; he kept it alive, seeing the complicated map of silver pipes and wires as a delicate surgical task. Sometimes, when the rain would start with the quick, static sound of an electric fuse, he'd push himself from under the truck, rising to watch the rain fall on all four sides of him, enclosing him in a soft blue world where he felt safe. He worked long hours until the sky turned orange and he returned home, still renting a room from his buddy Ryan.

On a Thursday, a man stepped into his office at Meineke. He told Caleb to shut up because he had some things to say. Caleb folded his arms, leaned back in his chair. "Do I owe you money? Did one of my guys screw you over?" The man told Caleb he wasn't there about his business. "Your business is a piece of shit," he said. Instead the man offered Caleb enough money to take a flight to Rhode Island the following week to attend a conference on theophostics—god *(theo)* and light *(phostics)*—where people came to be delivered from phobias, addictions, disorders, post-traumatic stress.

Caleb told the man he didn't want his money. The man left it anyway. An envelope of cash. The man told Caleb he needed help. Many years later, Caleb would say that this man was sent by God.

At the time, Caleb owed money for rent but he did what the man said and traveled to Rhode Island anyway. At a session, the leader fluttered her hands around Caleb and told him he was holding on to darkness. She brought Caleb to the center of the room. He stood under fluorescent lights, bowed his head. "Have you ever heard anyone pray in tongues?" the woman said.

"No, ma'am, I haven't."

She prayed in tongues, under her breath, reminding Caleb of those languages he'd never understood in the Middle East and Afghanistan. "Now, Caleb, do you believe in Jesus Christ?"

"Well, sure." He was born into a family who spoke of God at warm meals.

"Close your eyes and tell me what you see."

"I see the back of my eyelids."

"Father, show him what he needs to see!"

And he could see all the way back to when he was thirteen years old. It started with the guys burning in the helicopter, and the flesh coming off their skin. The day his ex-wife, Allyson, called him a murderer. The Black Thing telling Caleb he needed to die. All the horrible things that had happened in his life.

"Do you want to keep all those memories?"

No.

Everything went black. He could remember what happened—he knew his friends had burned and died—but he couldn't feel it. The emotion was gone.

Caleb looked at the silent, weeping crowd. A gathering of people also seeking help in this world. "I'm only twenty-five years old," Caleb told them, "but I feel like an old man." He wept too. Something he'd never done in public view.

The group's leader encouraged Caleb to talk in detail about the war, his dead buddies, and the apparitions that followed. A Vietnam veteran named Troy was in the audience, listening. When it was over, Troy introduced himself as a healer who sees and speaks healing to the deep hurts in the hearts of men. He had small, dark eyes. After Vietnam, he served twenty years as a firefighter and nineteen months as a trauma paramedic on combat posts in Afghanistan.

"Theophostics gets the little thing," he said, "but it's not going to make the big things go away."

Troy said he knew how to get rid of the big thing. The thing that was following Caleb home from the war.

"Society thinks PTSD cannot be healed," Troy said, "but society is wrong."

Troy described a place in South Georgia where the layer between heaven and earth is very thin. He'd traveled there two years ago to get rid of the Black Thing. He wished he'd done it earlier. "It's called deliverance," he said. "It works wonders." Troy offered to stop by Caleb's home and drive him to Portal. He'd take him through deliverance.

"Other veterans had done it," he said. "More are going to do it."

Troy showed up at Caleb's house the next day and unloaded a bundle of stakes from the trunk of his car. He wrote Scripture on their sides. Longhand with a permanent marker.

"You don't have to be this formal," he said, "this is just how I do it."

And he drove the stakes into the ground. "Now," he said, "nothing demonic can come on this property."

A week later, they drove together to Portal. Two hundred miles of night road while Troy spoke quietly of demons.

The town was no town at all really. A region of pine and dust and a violent history where turpentine hunters once distilled resin, and woodriders with bush knives hacked at undisciplined workers until they bled like hogs.

Off Highway 26, down a long washboard dirt road, Troy pulled up to a trailer where a minister and his wife lived alone.

They sat Caleb down in a room and all these Christian people surrounded him in foldout chairs. No one said anything. They were writing things down on pieces of paper.

Then one by one, they all said something was trying to kill Caleb. They got images, visions. They described his wrists bloody and wrapped in barbed wire. They described a sword coming for his heart. They said he was tied down to a railroad track and the train was coming. "I see a Destroyer," a man said, "in the form of a buffalo, trying to kill Caleb."

The minister saw an angel fighting the Destroyer. The angel was worn out and tired and all the hair had been ripped out of its head.

Caleb felt a burning sore rip open on the back of his neck. It felt as if the flesh was coming off and something was being pulled up his spine toward the burning. They prayed for the blood of Jesus. He could feel hot Jesus blood coming down over his face. Everyone in the room started freaking out. A glowing thing moved down his legs. They said they'd never seen that before.

The minister reached his hands into the air and closed his eyes. "Caleb," he said, "you have a reason to be alive."

Part III

HOW TO KILL
AN INVISIBLE ENEMY

Portal, Georgia, which lies between Statesboro and Swainsboro, has 562 people, one streetlight, one restaurant called Pepper Jack's, and a beauty pageant for infants called Baby Miss Turpentine. Dead armadillos are all over the road, shining dull the way I imagine diamonds look when pulled from the earth.

The minister and his wife, Tim and Katie Mather, Caleb's in-laws, perform deliverance in a building called the Covenant Bible Institute, next to the Portal Church of God and two gas stations, off a street called Railroad. The institute is dry and full of sun and looks like a colorless Pizza Hut. Tim and Katie don't actually hold service in a church, they gather at home, underground cells, a thing inspired by a fear of End Times, the Battle of Armageddon in the deserts of the Middle East.

In Portal there are dirt roads with signs pointing down more dirt roads. Most of them say CHURCH. Some of them are handwritten, some of them are fresh, industrial, but in most cases there is no church. LIFE IS SHORT. ETERNITY ISN'T. I WOULDN'T BE CAUGHT DEAD WITHOUT JESUS. GO TO CHURCH OR THE DEVIL WILL GET

YOU. PRAYER IS THE KEY TO UNLOCK JESUS. FOR THE HOPELESS
JESUS IS THE ONLY HOPE. YOU THINK IT'S HOT OUT HERE? TRY
HELL. BE HAPPY WITH YOURSELF. GOD LOVES YOU. COME IN, GOD
HAS A PLAN FOR YOU. YOU HAVE ONE NEW FRIEND REQUEST FROM
JESUS. ACCEPT? REJECT?

Tim and Katie live in a trailer fifteen minutes outside Portal.
It's a double wide, down four dirt roads, past a bullet-holed sign
that says Church, in the middle of a field they claim was once an
ocean. Fossils were dug from the ground; polished remains of giant
sharks and things with necks longer than a house. Eden says it was
the Flood.

No neighbors in view of their house. Only an abandoned building half eaten by vines.

Caleb says ninety-nine percent of people who come to the
trailer return to the trailer.

After Caleb gets his kids, Isabel and Isaac, settled, he puts me
in the windowless guest room with thin floral sheets and a porcelain angel. The angel has her hands raised in a nice way but her lips
are painted wrong. They are on the side of her face, near the cheek,
looking more wound than lip.

The minister is watching TV in the living room, on a leather
chair with gold trim and a foldout footrest, demanding things from
his wife, Katie. She didn't buy the right ice cream. He wanted vanilla
but not the kind with all the fruit in it. Katie looks around fifty
years old and has long blond hair that falls to her hips. Her shirt
says WILD WEST and her boots click softly on the blue linoleum.
The kitchen is a spread of raw ingredients waiting to be cooked.

The minister unpauses the TiVo. "We have visitors here all the
time," he says. He doesn't turn his neck but moves his entire torso
in my direction. He has small blue eyes like badly sewn buttons.
Hands big enough to grip a watermelon. "It's like a hotel. Help
yourself to anything." A dusty copy of the *Virginian* is propped

under the yellow glow of a rawhide lamp. He rocks slowly, watching an old Western on a flat-screen TV. His face breaks into a wide grin and the yellow ceiling light spills onto his forehead, making him glow along with the screen.

The trailer is blessed. The minister blesses all houses before he moves in. Words for him, once said, don't perish, but live on, in the plywood boards of his home, in the carpet, in the water he drinks. He uses the word *divorce* as an example. He says it quietly, with his hands over his mouth. He doesn't want the house to hear.

He blesses water and says the water that is blessed looks different under a microscope than the water that is cursed.

On the day the minister was outside feeding the chickens and came back inside to find his wife gone, a pot boiling, he was sure that God had come—taken his wife and left him. He got down on his knees and felt the first whimperings of despair.

There are photos of Roy Rogers in the bathroom and a saddle in the living room.

While Caleb watches TV with the minister I wander outside, onto the porch, where a woman's drinking something yellow, wearing sweatpants and a sweatshirt. She introduces herself as Pam. She's forty years old and she's "the adopted child." Pam followed the minister's family to Georgia from their previous home in upstate New York. She lives in Portal now. Her body spills from the chair. I hear her breathe. Some of her hair is curly and some straight. She kills ants with her feet.

"I worked at AT&T for twenty years," Pam says. "Nothing to write home about."

The minister has four children and fourteen grandchildren. They all live in Portal. His oldest child lives a dirt road away. It's a Saturday, and by late afternoon all fourteen grandkids, ranging from two months to nine years, are in the yard, jumping on the trampoline, screaming, running naked. One pisses on the ground, facing me, as close as possible without hitting my feet. Another picks ants out of the portable swimming pool and eats them. A redheaded nine-year-old named Amaryllis comes up to me and opens her mouth. I feed her.

Then there's the child that they say is different from the others. She does not talk, she moans. She always appears to be drowning, looking up while her eyes pool with light. Her hands are small white moths roaming the curves of her mother's body. Her mother is married to the minister's only son. She tells me she doesn't believe in autism.

A few veterans wander the yard fixing cars: Iraq, Somalia, Vietnam.

A hundred yards out, past the lawn chairs facing nowhere, past the pool full of dead ants, past the fallen children's toys, the grass turns to field, boulders break from the ground, and sunflowers stand leaning like the silhouettes of men. The field darkens at the curve of the earth, until it is eaten by the sky.

Out there, a dog, big as a colt and matted like it's just been put through the wash, is digging. He and the minister's dog Hoss make love at night, and everyone can hear their violence made public by the clear air. Hoss comes home in the morning, bloody and smiling.

Black clouds rise over the eastern sky and Pam takes me inside where the air is dense with the smell of butter and children. The minister's wife cuts lasagna into neat squares and passes them among us. The children sit at a long oak table, the adults in the living room.

The lights flicker and moan and one of them dies in a quiet flash.

Ice cream is passed. The power goes out. The trailer shakes with thunder. The children scream on cue and the mothers laugh, lighting candles. The men put on work boots and head outside. Lightning made a gash in the earth, they report. Smoke rises from the ground and hail replaces rain.

I ask Katie if we need to worry about anything.

I feel the room go quiet behind me and when I turn around everyone is staring at me, forks stopped in midair, mouths open.

"Georgia gets tornados," she says, crossing her arms. "But this property doesn't." I excuse myself to the living room. They stop talking to me. I pick the smallest infant to hold. It has blue eyes, same as all the others.

Caleb joins me and touches my back. "Don't worry," he says. "They're not being rude."

The baby is as fat and pale and hairless as a baby could possibly be. It crawls along the floor using only its front arms to slide forward.

"It's just that they don't think they're talking to you. They think they're talking to your demons."

Morning, and the television is the trailer's bright center. The minister rocks in his chair, whistling with a wide mouth.

Katie's drinking tea on the couch next to him with her legs crossed, hunched over a book called *When Heaven Invades Earth,* purple clouds and a lightning bolt on the cover. I step into the room and they tell me Caleb's gone to work on the vehicles. Faraway towns, asking for money. "He'll be back."

The light is filtered through dark curtains. I sit down on the couch across from Katie and look at the minister. "Caleb told me to talk to you." The television goes dark. "About what?" he says. He was a preacher for twenty-nine years and his voice is thick and cool as a bite of peach. Katie puts a pen in her book and leaves the room.

"If you really want to know," he says. "I've written six books on demonic bondage. I'll let you borrow one if you want." He lifts himself out of the rocking chair, using both hands to leverage his weight, and disappears into his bedroom. The door opens just enough to reveal a wide bed burdened with yellowing pillows. One of his granddaughters reposes naked on the bed. She holds both her feet at her ankles and spreads them winglike, lifting them outward and upward. Her head falls back in a quick flourish and she springs to her feet, dancing, using the mattress as a trampoline to propel her frame upward. She lands and balances herself, elegantly, a ballerina before the onslaught of applause.

The minister's son walks into the room. "Who are you?" he asks.

"I'm Caleb's friend," I say, not wanting to explain.

"Caleb has friends?"

The minister returns with a book called *Prophetic Deliverance: The Missing Ministry in the Church of God*. On the cover a sunset breaks foamy clouds. The book is self-published and the category is spiritual warfare.

I flip through the pages. Definitions of demons. Origins of demons. Names of demons. It's mostly anecdotes about the minister's encounters with demons. The whole religion came to him in a prophecy while mowing the lawn six years ago in Elmira, New York.

"How many have you brought through deliverance?"

"I stopped counting at five thousand."

All deliverance ministries believe people are in bondage to a pattern of sin. Trauma is a doorway through which demons can pass. It grew out of Pentecostalism, a movement often traced to a run-down Apostolic Faith Mission on Azusa Street in Los Angeles, birthed in 1906 by the fervent demands of the one-eyed preacher William J. Seymour, son of slaves. Three waves of Pentecostalism followed. Many third-wave Pentecostals assign a demon or a corps of demons to geopolitical units in the world.

"One of the biggest problems with prophetic deliverance," the minister says, "or so I've been told by religious minds, is that it's too simple. We had one woman who used some severe language after hers. She stomped her feet and started yelling, 'I'm so fucking mad. I'm so fucking angry.' The birthing process, it just takes a minute. It doesn't take hours."

"Do you think everyone has a demon?"

"Yes. It's usually people who've been through traumatic experiences." He throws a thumb at the place where Katie had been sitting. "She experienced trauma that could only be fixed with deliverance. But the trauma can be small."

"Can I observe a session?"

The minister says no, that won't be happening. He reaches for his lemonade. The chair groans beneath his weight. "It's too dangerous." He gulps, sighs. "The demons can transfer. Once we forgot to put protection over the cars out in the parking lot and the demons tore up four vehicles in a row. It's no joke."

"I asked what would happen if I went through deliverance."

He tells a story about a depressed Protestant. Protestants don't believe God can inhabit the body, and deliverance requires this belief to work properly. Eventually the Protestant told the minister that he converted but must have lied because during the session the man started gagging, making terrible retching sounds like his insides were coming out. He put his hands on his knees and coughed up a cloud of black flies.

Two months later he was in jail for armed robbery.

"How much does it cost to get the demons out?"

"God said if I ever charged you, he'd kill me."

For a while, the Mathers gave deliverance to anyone who asked, but Tim heard stories of people going crazy, ending up in jail. Now it's required that anyone who receives deliverance spend three days in Portal. He calls it a deliverance retreat. It costs $199, which includes food, housing, a demon workbook, classes on spiritual warfare, and a thirty-minute exorcism. Each retreat has a fifteen-person limit and everyone's required to have read Tim Mather's book. They're thinking of buying a building where they can bring people through deliverance on a regular schedule, but for now they go anywhere there's space: the trailer, empty stores in Portal, abandoned buildings, their daughters' houses, the Covenant Bible Institute.

"The best way to understand deliverance," he says, "is from a military standpoint." He starts equating prophecy with military intelligence and deliverance with boot camp. "Boot camp is where civilians are transformed into soldiers. It's uncomfortable and unsettling but you come out of there a warrior, well-equipped and unafraid."

At one point he thought of calling it death camp because you would be dying for Christ. But then he realized the name would scare people.

Tim reaches for the remote. "Well, it's a good thing I have a TV. It's my only connection to the real world."

The phone rings. He answers, listens, sighs. He presses the receiver to his chest and bows his head. Katie looks up from her place in the kitchen. They embrace in the light near the porch doors. Katie leans her head back and closes her eyes to a wide beam of sunlight.

"A poverty demon just arrived in Portal," he says.

Tim and Katie met as ten-year-olds at Bible camp and went together as much as ten-year-olds could. They lost touch, found each other again. Another Bible camp, another town. They were sixteen and played in the high school Gospel band. Three years later, they married, and after they married, Tim enrolled at Toccoa Falls College in Georgia. After a semester and a half, he quit. It was a recession and they had three kids. The military was Tim's last-ditch effort to get a job.

He was stationed in the small town of Minot, North Dakota. One day a traveling evangelist named Bill Putnam made his way through town to visit the soldiers. They gathered at the Christian and Missionary Alliance Church and Tim confessed to Mr. Putnam that he'd been having some bowel problems. Mr. Putnam told Tim not to worry—he knew just the thing. Mr. Putnam placed both his hands on Tim's head and told a group of demons to get off his tongue. Tim didn't like the idea of demons living in his tongue, but then his mouth filled with saliva and he felt them leave. Swallowing, Tim wrote in *Prophetic Deliverance*, never felt so good. They stayed for seven years, and an ex-pastor took Tim through deliverance in 1980. At the time, he was in his late thirties and feared darkness. Now, when it's completely dark, he can walk out the door of his house and across the yard, down the lane, past horses and the animals in the woods.

Tim always believed he saw things in the dark. It began with shadows and faces and then the faces began to speak and then the ghosts stayed even with the lights on. Each night he said a sinner's prayer and waited for morning to come. Otherworldly creatures stalked his bedroom. His first demonic memory comes from childhood, when a purple frog demon sat on his head. It came back every night and slipped beneath warm covers to join him in his dreams. His parents sometimes found him shivering on the porch in his underwear.

In his early years, he made money as a janitor for his father's church, mopping floors, scrubbing the bathrooms. Voices and footsteps in the silence. Demons enveloped him. The faucets ran. He locked all the doors. He played records to cover the voices.

One day a formless ghost appeared at his bedside. It floated and teased and then it attacked by sucking all the air out of his lungs.

Tim determined the acts of the demon to be torture and declared war.

In the military, the hauntings increased. Tim was a policeman assigned to guard an intercontinental ballistic missile site. He was with his buddy and they saw something running in the dark. It came for them. This figure ripped through their truck. The radio cracked and the lights died and the thing was gone.

The minister found comfort in the writer Stephen King, who he thought knew more about the spiritual realm than any Christian. He'd read on the back of one of King's books: "When I was young, I worried about my sanity a lot." He called the author an ungodly man.

After his deliverance, Tim started attending classes at the local Bible college, and leading air force guys to the Lord. One night they ended up with almost a hundred airmen in the room. Tim and Katie discipled the men. Prayed for the men. Delivered the men. Demons manifested. Screaming and swearing and puking and levitating. Vile talk. The airmen spoke in demon voices.

Katie was delivered for the second time in May 1993. When she was a kid she was raped by the older boys in her neighborhood. She didn't tell Tim about the older boys until eighteen years into their marriage when he asked about her darkest secret and she punched him in the face. She split his lip. He'd been picking at sore spots, old wounds, brokenness.

Tim suspected a second demon and called on his father to organize a session. They circled Katie and aked the Holy Spirit to reveal her demon. Katie waited for the news. Tim's father grew anxious. He did not want to reveal the name of the demon. Finally he said, "It's the demon of whoredom."

When the words reached her, Katie started gagging. Not just dry heaves—she was choking and she couldn't breathe. Tim wasn't going to let this demon take his wife. He stood up and commanded the demon to say its name. And in a deep, raspy voice, Katie bellowed: *I am Control.*

Her real name is Kathleen, but after the demon left, God told her to change it to Katie.

The Mathers came to Portal in 1999 because God told them to come. Tim was mowing the lawn when it happened. The voice of God came down to him. He looked at a map and realized Portal was not a town where any man would ever wish to live. That's exactly why God wanted him to come to Portal. Nothing would ever happen in that town. It was off the radar of high-ranking demons, he believed.

But still, Tim resisted the idea. He'd been preaching for twenty-nine years and didn't want his preacher's life to end. Corpse dreams haunted his sleep. In the dreams he was standing on the street, looking at a pile of dead bodies. He grabbed a body, pulled it out, set it on the curb. He did this over and over again. Piling corpses. Row after row. When he tired of this, he sat down and wept. After whispering to the Lord, after asking what to do, one of the corpses moaned. It got up suddenly and it moved around and it looked at him. You're alive? Tim said. The corpse nodded.

Tim decided the corpses were all the church people he needed to revive through deliverance and he decided on a title for himself: Harvester of the Dead.

Tim gathered with pastors and prayed over cities; fought and lost against angels of death; dealt with demons in front of large crowds; witnessed a batlike creature standing behind a woman who feared everything; encountered a barking man with a demon named Unteachable; found a woman whose tongue was so twisted she couldn't say *my body belongs to Jesus*; and entered the home of a worn, bag-eyed girl named Sally who cut herself bloody while a group of pastors blew shofar.

On a mission to Africa, the whole Mather clan was spreading word about demons. They saw a woman manifest in the streets.

A gaunt bishop grabbed ahold of her, hauled her onstage, and started banging the woman's head against the ground. The minister walked up to the bishop and said, "Can you punch a demon?" The bishop said no, they're ethereal. "Then why are you punching this woman?" All these years he'd been hitting people to get the demon out. Tim whispered, "Would you like the demon to go?" Her eyes spun like a slot machine.

On a recent visit to the trailer, Tim's mother reported back to the Mather family that she'd traveled into the spirit realm, floated over the property, and looked around.

A battlefield, she said. All these dead bodies rotting in the grass.

The minister thinks each of his four children should have four children and that each of those children should have four children. I've seen him move his arms like a conductor and say, "Be fruitful and multiply and fill the earth and subdue it and have dominion over the fish of the sea and over the birds of the heavens and over every living thing that moves on the earth!"

Eden is childless and therefore different from the others.

We're in the yard—wet, green, and bright. Pam, the adopted child, is at the porch table, moving her fingers on the plastic like someone tracing the shapes of small clouds. Eden calls her parents politically incorrect. "I just taught my mom to be more hospitable when guests arrive. You know: Do you want water? Do you need anything? But we're all very close and give each other permission to speak into one another's lives. Sometimes it's too much." Eden smiles, plays with her wedding ring, twirls it. "My father, especially, scares a lot of people. He can look at you and he can see your darkness. But don't worry, he doesn't really look unless you give him permission."

Eden gathers children in her arms, and leaves to make sandwiches.

The yard is full of growlers and men, all of them working with

Caleb on his business, holding beer cans to the sun. Among them is Troy, the Vietnam veteran who brought Caleb to Portal for deliverance. A big man with lines on his face rough as a dry ditch. His nose curves toward the earth, as if dripping, too many days standing on his feet in the heat and wet of the jungle.

"What demon did you have?"

"Devil of Religion," Troy says. "They found thorns on my feet. Then later I come home and I find a giant Buddha sitting in my house."

I tell Troy I'm reading Tim's book.

"What they don't tell you is skip the first half," he says. "The second half's the only half that matters."

Mud-covered men take tools to a steaming growler. Children dance about it in strange worship.

"Growler burst into flames," Caleb says. He walks toward me with an oily rag on his shoulder. "Max cracked his beer to put the fire out."

"I could of pissed on it," Max says.

"Marine," Caleb adds, as if to define a species.

The men grunt and point, exchanging deep-throated laughs.

Max was in the Marine Corps Reserve's Anti-Terrorism Unit and is a veteran of the war in Somalia. Caleb hired him to work in the factory. He's blond and has a peanut-shaped head, peppers his talk with ah-shits. Born in Vidalia, a town in central Georgia known for its onions, Max is now divorced and twenty-five and has a three-year-old girl at home. The skull tattoo on his forearm says, UNITED STATES MISGUIDED CHILDREN. "Stands for United States Marine Corps," he says, covered in grease, checking something in the vehicle's insides. "I never went to Iraq, but that's the war we talked about in Somalia." As if to prove his point, he shows me a photograph he keeps in his wallet: men by a swimming pool, and beyond that, red earth.

Everyone heads back to the trailer for sandwiches. I ask Max if we can talk. Caleb told me Max might kill himself because his two best friends killed themselves after they got out of the military.

Max doesn't answer. He's too busy pawing the beer cooler's tepid water. Pam, the adopted child, is still sitting at the porch table, picking lint off her sweater. I sit next to her. The rooster and his cohort of chickens sleep in a pile under the minister's truck.

I wait until Max manages a Bud Light from the cooler, gleaming like caught trout.

"What was Somalia like?" I say.

He brings the bottle to his lips but hesitates before drinking. "In Somalia there were people without arms running across the border. Christians. Muslims. I have no idea."

He's been out two years, started in August of '06, and in February '07, he says, shit hit the fan. "They ordered us to go to this airstrip just across the border. Three planes landed. We didn't know about the mission because we were just there for security. Next thing, the marine air crew is up on the intercom, saying *stand by for fire*. Out of nowhere three enemy planes landed. The gunship opened. We were in a truck with a bunch of kids from South Georgia. One of them—poor guy—he was sitting next to me and he was the first to fire. The Russian version of a grenade launcher shot off the bottom of his rifle. It fired and exploded about five meters near me. Killed some guys. A piece of it came and sliced me up. Hit me right here on the collarbone."

He speaks quietly and with mumbled words. There are details I miss, sentences swallowed.

"That was pretty much it. Lasted about two hours. There for six months, saw nothing. Then, out of nowhere, everything went wrong."

Between Pam's thumb and forefinger is a black ball of lint, small and robust as a tick. I cup my hand over my mouth so Pam can't hear. I ask, "Do you believe in deliverance?"

"Fuck no," Max says. "Creepy shit." He has a quiet, uncomfortable laugh, as if something he's not used to feeling in his lungs. "Satan would blow fireballs out of my ass."

Max doesn't want to talk about his dead friends. Instead he says Caleb once rode a C-130 plane into Vietnam, penetrating its wilds to save American POWs left over from the war. He says Caleb has been in South America, traveling by night, trying to kill Hugo Chávez. Max drinks five beers and says he knows a lot about trucks. Max says he's trying to get a job at AutoZone. He doesn't want to talk about Corey and the other guy whose name he swallowed up before I could hear. Corey was the kid he met on the bus to boot camp, the kid he ended up with in the desert of Somalia, same platoon. Corey's brother died in a car wreck. He was in Somalia when it happened. He was on leave to attend his brother's funeral when he shot himself. "I don't understand why he didn't call me," Max says. "He was my best friend. I didn't get the chance to talk him out of it."

Pam puts a hand flat on the table. "I'm getting milk," she says. "We need milk. Does anyone want any milk or anything else that can be gotten at the store?"

"We don't want any," Max says.

"I'm going to the store. Does anyone need any milk?" she asks again.

"No, thanks, Pam."

"Do you think anyone inside wants milk?"

"You could ask," I say.

"Yes." Pam pauses, looks off at the field, walks to the door with her back bent, rising slowly, poking her head into the house. Out come the minister's bothered groans.

She walks past us to her Camaro, turning to look back just once, showing us her eyes, as if the only thing she wanted in life were to be given the smallest task to complete. The car idles. She does not return for many hours, longer than one would need to get milk, and when she does finally return, she slams her bulldog frame against the sliding glass door. We are all inside. In her hands: a carton of two percent. Gripping it like a football, thumping it slowly and rhythmically against the glass. "Will someone let her in?" the minister says, but Pam enters on her own. "What is it, Pam?"

"I saw something," she says, pointing and bouncing, tripping on her shoe. Sweat pools in the curve above her lip. "It walked across the road, right in front of my car. I almost hit it."

The minister is half listening, watching a movie in which men are torn apart by dinosaurs.

"It was like bigfoot," she says. "It had horns. A silver back."

The minister recommends a glass of water. A small child lingers in the hallway. He tells the child, "Give Pam a hug."

The child shows his teeth. "I don't want to," he says.

I help Pam with some water and we retreat to the porch, where the sky is livid and smoke corkscrews from the burn pile.

"What was it?"

She shakes her head and settles into her chair in the manner of a roosting hen. "They want to be seen," she says.

At some late hour I find the minister roaming the halls in his floppy nightshirt, moving around like a jellyfish. "I might send a demon into your room tonight," he said. The comment is followed by laughter. That night, in the windowless guest room, I let the lamp burn until morning and keep my limbs close on the hard, skinny gurney bed. Field mice move around the bedroom's shadows. The pillow's fabric has yellow flowers. I wonder if they think I'm infecting the room. They could see a demon on me and strangle me. In Fra Angelico's *The Last Judgment*, the demon has black hair and red eyes. Sometimes the devil appeared as a medieval bestiary of snakes, dragons, lions, goats. Bats were birds of the devil. Demons were toads and toadlike creatures. Often the devil resided in the body of a pig. *Le lupeux*, a night phantom of the Norman marshes, has birdlike aspects. Demons had membranous bat wings. Scorpion tails. Often the devil had red skin or red hair or red clothes or skin that burned with red flames. They carried tools of torture. For three centuries the devil was depicted as a beautiful young girl from the country.

Caleb's twenty-four-year-old brother, John, just redeployed to Iraq and has been struggling. For the first time, Caleb told me, he's been having trouble dealing with combat. On his most recent deployment, John helped four injured Iraqi soldiers by wrapping their wounds, giving them water, and listening to their stories. He knew the color of their eyes, the curve of their noses, and a few weeks later, after they were released from the medics, he shot them during a crossfire. Now he sees their faces everywhere he goes, at night and in his dreams. He's thinking too much about the enemies. How what once was abstract now has a human face. He can't pull the trigger. He misses on purpose, sweats under his helmet.

Isaac, the five-year-old, asks Caleb about killing people. It's my fifth day at the trailer and we're all on lawn chairs, Caleb with his legs wide, a shirt draped over his shoulders, hand scratching his neck. It's stiff and tendoned as a celery stalk. Isaac's curled in the grass. The other children run circles in the yard. Caleb doesn't lie. He tells Isaac it's Uncle John's duty.

"Dad, I want to go to Iraq."

"Isaac," Caleb says, "you're really not old enough yet."

Caleb leans back and crosses his arms behind his head. "I think the only way we're going to get you there is to FedEx you."

In the evening Isaac tells Isabel about what their dad said. They find a box and Isaac curls inside it. Isabel tucks newspaper in the spaces his body doesn't fill.

Later Caleb finds Isaac in the box, and he rips it open. Isaac says he was waiting to get FedExed to Iraq, just like his dad told him.

A few years ago Katie stopped keeping records of those who went through deliverance. "I don't need that darkness on file," she says, as if the darkness of the notes were a literal thing that would sustain life in her drawers.

"Sometimes Caleb will send someone but they don't have to tell us," she says. "It might be something that comes up in deliverance. We don't have to know about the war to save them from it. Tim is a veteran. He served six years in the air force. There are many veterans that we've brought through deliverance, from the current wars, but also from past wars, people that are our age and older. Veterans as far back as, well, who knows? We've even done some from the Korean War. They've been over sixty years old. We've had lots of Vietnam vets. We just delivered a couple in Special Forces. Then another woman who's a veteran and her husband who's now in Afghanistan."

"And you believe they all have the Destroyer?"

"What would be a typical personality that would be serving in the military?" Katie seems to be figuring this out as we speak. "I'm thinking especially of Special Forces. Usually those ones have a Destroyer on them because their jobs are dangerous. The enemy uses your tendencies against you. That's something we've been looking into and thinking about."

I ask about Caleb's theory that the demons would transfer to me if I spoke to any other veterans about their trauma.

"If you're in contact with those who are suicidal," she says, "you can pick up what are called familiar spirits. They can attach to you. It's basic spiritual warfare. We do it every day. It's from Ephesians: The breastplate of righteousness, the belt of truth, the shoes of readiness, the gospel of peace, the shield of faith, and the helmet of salvation. The sword of the spirit is the word of God and it aims to do damage against the kingdom of the enemy. God is stronger than what the enemy can throw at you. You are able to crush all the fiery darts."

"What about suicide bombers? Is it the same drive?"

"They aren't killing themselves out of hopelessness. They're killing themselves out of religious belief. It's a religious demon. At least they have something to believe in. A lot of Christians here don't really believe in the power of God. A lot of people who label themselves as Christians function more like unbelievers, not like heathens, but they don't believe that God is bigger than their problems. They treat Christianity like insurance to keep them out of hell. But it seems like people who would martyr themselves to kill other people are the most dangerous of all." She pauses and then says, "I attempted suicide when I was twelve. I punished myself. I wished I was dead. After deliverance, that all went away. Remarkably, it went away. For twelve years I was plagued with suicidal thoughts. Or I would think, what if my car went off the road and hit that tree?"

"What stopped you?"

"I would never kill myself as a believer. I would just pray not to wake up in the morning."

All day Pam sits quietly in the lawn watching the field. Every day there's obsessive talk of demons. No one seems to mind that I'm there and so I stay ten days, eleven days, twelve. Katie warns never to ask for anything from her. "You know where the cabinets are. Help yourself to milk. Help yourself to bread."

On a night out for Mexican food at a place called Sombrero's I'm the only one not wearing cowboy boots. When I mention this to Eden she says she knows of a place. She says she likes the ones that have colors—blue, snakeskin, and white.

Caleb doesn't drink alcohol. Caleb turns a little red in the face and stuffs chew in his mouth, repeating the word *horchata*. "Horchata, have you ever had horchata?" In the military they gave him speech therapy to erase his southern accent because no one could understand him over the intercom, but it's reclaiming him. His stomach hurts and he picks up a slice of lemon and eats the whole thing.

He crosses his legs and talks about skirts. He hates skirts. "You know what I think about those Frenchies?" he says. "I think they're a bunch of skirts."

"I've got a joke," Max says. "So Sigmund Freud is eating dinner with his wife and she says, 'Honey, please pass the salt,' and he says, 'I hate you, you fucking stupid bitch.'"

Eden dips her finger in salt and licks. "I don't get it."

"Yeah, what're you talking about?" Caleb says.

"Never mind," Max says.

"By the way," Caleb says to me. "My ex-girlfriend Krissy called. She never calls. She hasn't called since we broke up three years ago." Caleb thinks it's a sign. He wants me to meet her. "Only thing is: she's totally insane." He reminds me about the gun she pulled on him.

Krissy doesn't want to talk to me, but days later she calls Caleb back and says she changed her mind. She wants to meet me at a diner in a town called Pooler, halfway between Portal and Savannah. The next afternoon I drive over alone. Krissy arrives straight from her job at the YMCA, wearing Lycra pants and a fleece sweater.

"I don't really want to talk to you," she says. "I don't want to think about those days." It's the first time she's talked about Caleb—about #146—with anyone, for years. "But I don't want anyone to ever go through what I had to go through with Caleb."

A thin-haired waitress, about eighty years old, hands us ketchup-stained plastic menus with photographs of food on their insides.

She wipes her hands on a tight blue button-up dress. It matches a tiny paper hat sitting atop her hair like a bluebird in its nest.

"So if you can help others understand what was happening to Caleb, what was going on in his brain, I'll tell you whatever you want." Krissy puts her hands together. She stays this way, gathering thoughts.

She says Caleb started waking up in the middle of the night and he'd tell her he was watching the crash. That Kip would come in the room and they would talk about the crash together. "Usually, it would be around one forty-six in the morning. Sometimes I'd wake up and Caleb wasn't in the bed. I would find him in another part of the house curled in the fetal position, rocking back and forth. Sometimes I'd wake up and hear him crying. What is it? I'd ask. Something always with Kip. Caleb believed that Kip was really there—that it wasn't just something he dreamed. I didn't see anything. But I knew he really believed it. I thought it was just PTSD."

Krissy balls up a napkin in her fist and presses it to her lips. "He'd have terrors," she says. "All of a sudden the light would switch." The napkin goes deeper into her mouth. "He'd literally just be sitting there, looking right at me, but it was like he didn't see me. He looked right through me. I'd try to talk to him but he wouldn't hear me. Then all of a sudden he'd be back. He'd shake his head and say, What just happened? Where am I?"

When Caleb and Krissy went to restaurants, he'd sit in the corner. He couldn't have his back to anyone. He'd say, If somebody walks in here to shoot up the place, I'll see it. I'll know what to do. He had a blueprint in his mind: Okay, if somebody comes in here to do something, I am going to flip this table. I'm going to grab this bottle here and be ready. Sometimes there would be nobody in the place.

On a weekend trip to Atlanta, Caleb and Krissy found themselves lost on a dark road. No one around. No idea how they'd gotten there. Caleb was driving. He had that faraway look. Krissy knew right away that it was Kip. She didn't realize until they merged back onto the highway, but she'd taken exit one forty-six. "Next thing we know the time is one forty-six in the morning."

I ask about the gun and Krissy says it was a birthday gift from Caleb. She says she never turned it on herself. "There were times he'd say he was going to kill himself. That's when I knew he was out of my control. I couldn't mention anything or it would go quickly from a small issue like doing the dishes to: I'm going to kill myself." She says this while slipping a purse strap over her arm. "I'm sorry, I don't really want to talk about this anymore." She walks away and then turns around. "You know, at the time, I was fighting thoughts of suicide myself. I'd never been like that before I met Caleb."

Kristina, Kip's old girlfriend, and Valarie, the woman who makes dinner for her dead husband, live in Savannah and I spend the day and a night there to talk to them. Valarie, when we meet, hardly speaks. When she does it seems painful, a voice from elsewhere that isn't really her own, like she hadn't said anything for weeks. Her hair is cut to her ears and parted very straight in the center. Instead of the thin spread of crow's-feet on the ends of her eyes, she has dimples, dents that are curved and deep.

Valarie worked for the National Guard and a few months later she was in Iraq. She met her husband, Chris, on the front lines. Valarie tells me stories about how they used to share sniper duty on rooftops. Caleb said they wouldn't take a shit without being ten feet from each other.

On leave at Hunter Army Airfield, Chris's friend called and asked if Chris could pick up a wedding dress for her in Mobile, Alabama. Chris didn't want to waste time driving, so he and two buddies used a military chopper to get the dress. On the way back, the chopper collided with an electrical tower. The men were found in contorted positions on the ground, the wedding dress caught like a web between stalks of wheat.

Many continue on like Valarie, quietly setting plates for loved ones. Their lives slip past statistics.

Kristina asks to meet at a bar called Kevin Barry's Irish Pub at ten in the morning on a Wednesday, and it's already full of women drinking. A girl in the back of the bar wearing a wifebeater, and another with purple nails, and one sitting with her arms to her side looking at a glass of rum.

On the second floor, in a high-ceiled room that's dark but full of amber light collecting in glasses, we sit at a table near a photograph of Kip, alongside photographs of the other seven Night Stalkers who died on Chinook 146 and the others who died in Afghanistan and those who died in Iraq and anyone who died in any wars with Americans in it. Where there are no photos, they're paintings, some gruesome—bodies ripped apart, men giving water to screaming men, a nameless coffin, an eagle crying. There's a section of the wall reserved for the victims of 9/11.

Kristina takes her shirt off. "Don't worry," she says, "I'm not going to show you my boobs." Underneath she has on a pink tank top with sparkle-written words. She lifts her elbow to her ear and below her armpit there's a chopper tattoo. It says EVIL EMPIRE in thick black letters. "That was the Chinook," she says. "The one he died on."

She knows a lot of military wives talking about their husbands as if they were invincible. "But the war is real, people really are dying. Then there's a lot of couples getting in fights over the phone. Yelling at each other. Hanging up. But you can't call back. As the wife, you can't call back." She and Kip had rules: No hanging up on each other. No hanging up without saying "I love you."

Kristina and her new husband almost divorced last year. He's an Army Ranger, and between deployments he wouldn't talk to her, he'd only play video games. He told her all the soldiers have to fill out a psych evaluation on the plane. On a scale of one to ten, how do you feel about this? Do you feel suicidal? Everyone fills out *I'm fine*, she says, because they just want to get home.

Kristina digs a manila folder out of her purse and sets it on the table. "I call this the Death Folder."

The Death Folder is full of photographs of Kip, letters from Kip, newspaper clippings about the crash, pages torn from magazines like *USA Today* and *U.S. News & World Report*. She hands me a photo of Kip, the last one they took of each other before he died. In the photo, they're lying on their stomachs in bed, shoulders pressed together, bending their heads just slightly to be sure to fit in the frame.

"It's military policy. He belongs to the government. So regardless of whether he was burned or shot or whatever, he's in a wooden box and that's that." Kristina points to the photograph of Kip on the wall. "I am sure he was badly burned and probably not recognizable, but at the same time I would have felt better seeing the body. Really *seeing* that he's not coming back." She takes the photograph, slips it back into the stack of clippings. "In my mind," she says, "there's always this weird lingering feeling that maybe he's not dead."

Kip Jacoby died the same day George W. Bush gave a thirty-minute speech at Fort Bragg about the War on Terror. "Like most Americans, I see the images of violence and bloodshed. Every picture is horrifying, and the suffering is real." A year before, Tami Silicio, a cargo worker, was fired for photographing flag-draped caskets filling a plane in Kuwait. Bush said the 1991 ban on photographing coffins and war casualties was a law that protected the privacy and dignity of the families. As of 2010, Americans may photograph flag-draped coffins but they may not photograph the bodies of dead American soldiers.

Some psychologists think it's better to see the body because the fantasy would be worse. It helps the victim recover. It's evidence that the dead are dead.

There are thousands of American graveyards in Europe, full of sprinklers and bone-white monuments, and miles of green rolling hills and pressed flags. We are here to symbolize America's commitment to good, they boast. There are no American graveyards in Iraq or Afghanistan. Iraq is the first American war in which all the bodies have been repatriated. American soldiers who died in the Korean War were buried in Korean soil near the battlefields where they died. But then later we decided to unearth them, bring them home. Vietnam is the same.

Bodies of dead Iraqis clot the Tigris while acres of U.S. military vehicles hit by IED explosions fill nameless desert graveyards. Like bodies, they are blown apart, burned, shattered, cracked, or seemingly disassembled into constituent parts. It was not men who died, they seem to say, but machines.

Until families complained, bodies flew home on commercial airliners: cold cargo stacked on Nike bags, a casket on a belt loader, a US Airways flight from Denver to Vegas. Now bodies are transported on military planes with escorts. At the airport, an honor guard moves the casket instead of a forklift.

And finally a question from the military for the parents of children who come back in pieces: If more were discovered and subsequently identified, would the mother or the father like those missing pieces returned?

For eight years, unwanted parts were incinerated and dumped in a landfill at the Dover Air Base mortuary. Gari-Lynn Smith, whose husband died in Iraq, said she didn't want the military putting her husband's body in the trash. Now mortuary affairs puts unwanted body parts in the ocean.

• • •

115

The rain from last night has ceased and pooled yellow along the driveway's ditched sides. The burn pile steams, always alive with smoke. The trailer seeps a green light. Caleb's lupine eyes watch from the framed darkness of the trailer doorway. He's been pacing the yard. I see his tracks, the ripped-up grass, the purple roots reaching upward. Now he's waiting in the doorway; arms gripping the frame. Insects go to the lantern to die, burning and perfuming the air. Moths float dustlike or pound themselves mad for light. The horizon is a long green glow dissolving to night.

Caleb walks about the kitchen looking like a bear just out of hibernation, slow to remember the world. His eyes turn to the field and then back to me.

"What did Krissy say?"

"She said you had PTSD."

"Krissy saw Kip just as well as I did."

"She didn't say."

"Did you hear about Pam? She was driving the other day and she saw this big huge ape thing cross the road. She described it: six-foot-five with a silver back. It ran past, kinda hunkered over. It looked like Bigfoot but with horns. She recognized immediately that it was a demon. I asked her, well, what do you think it is? She said: *angel of poverty*."

I ask what he thinks I would see.

"With you, I don't know. There are a lot of people who see stuff who aren't Christians. The only difference is how you interpret it. If you aren't Christian then it's very scary to see them. Maybe it would appear in your dreams or you'd sense it, or it'd appear right in front of you like an animal running by."

He crosses his arms and shakes his head. "Did Tim tell you what happened?" Caleb says. "I can't believe you missed it."

He starts to tell me about a flashback, or a nightmare, in which a giant buffalo threatened to attack the trailer, and as he tells it I imagine he exists in the world the way trees do, quietly through wars and upheaval and love, something no longer part of time but burdened with its secrets.

At ten minutes to three in the morning, Caleb says, he woke with a stiff back and wide eyes, looking to the left and to the right. His children were screaming, and they never scream. He gathered them in his arms and brought them to Eden. "Something is here," he said, dropping a child on each side of his wife. The porch door slammed and he ran to it. He looked out the window. The field was dark, almost as if a curtain had been pulled over it. The green trailer light bathed tall stalks of grass. Solid like a wall.

The foliage moved and a spotlight appeared in the field. Eden's mother, Katie, in her nightgown, arms spread like a scarecrow. Something's going on, she said, something's here.

Caleb says he jogged around to the front of the house and there was a thing standing in the driveway, waiting for him, right where the hump is between the driveway and the dirt road. Right on the line. "My best guess is that this thing was six-foot-five. It was dark. I couldn't figure out what it was. It had something crazy on its head. At this point, I think it's a real person. I start yelling at this thing, throwing rocks at it, thinking I'm going to confront it." He walked toward it to get a better look. "This thing, it's like a man's body but it's got hoofed feet and it's got a buffalo head. He's got this big buffalo head on him with two little horns. So it hits me: this is a demon, not a person."

Caleb shows me how the horns curved on the buffalo by drawing them on his head with his hands.

"Three in the morning?"

He looks surprised. "It's when all the shit happens."

Eden steps into the kitchen with a towel wrapped around her head, freshly showered.

Caleb reaches his hand in the air above his head as if grasping for high fruit. "Are the kids both out?"

"I was just there," Eden says.

"See if Isabel is having a bad dream."

Eden leaves. She walks down the hallway.

"So I start taking authority over this thing," he says, "praying against it, and I command it to leave. In the past, because of my authority, it would have been gone like this: *snap*. But it didn't leave. This is the first time it didn't leave. But you know, it kinda had to leave, and so it just turns around and shrugs its shoulders like this." Caleb turns his back to me, and then slowly gives me longing eyes over his left shoulder. "It kind of had an attitude to it, you know? It walked a little ways down the road, ten paces or so, then stopped and turned around and gave me a look like this: What're you going to do now? So I chased its little ass down the road. You know that shack next to the trailer? It made a left and went through the wall. That's when I stopped. That's when the dogs started going ape shit. They were howling. Tim has never heard them howl."

Caleb takes a hissing slurp of Coke and rubs damp hands on his jeans. "It's the first time since combat that I've felt there was a real threat."

"How do you make sense of it?" I ask.

"Remember that thing that came into my room and said, *I will kill you if you proceed*? That was him." He puts the Coke down and grips the sink, hangs his head, and stares into the drain.

"It makes me feel better that it was so big. I can't fight something that big. It's been upping its game each time. But I'm okay with it. I like the idea of fighting a big, terrible enemy."

I call a clinical neuropsychologist at Fort Bragg whose job is to evaluate the psychological health of soldiers entering the Special Forces. When I tell her about the demons, she asks that I not use her name.

"If he comes into the military, fine," she tells me, "and leaves messed up, that's completely understandable. That's completely normal. That's a normal reaction to an abnormal event." The military, she reminds me, is an organization that trains people how to kill other people. "If you arrive with problems, then you're going to end up a lot worse than when you came in. These people, their resources are capped out when they see their friends blown up."

I'd read about a video game therapy for soldiers with PTSD called Virtual Iraq, where scientists have reduced flashbacks by up to 80 percent in some veterans. The program is a modified version of the video game Full Spectrum Warrior, but instead of watching a screen, patients put on a pair of goggles and a helmet to find themselves strolling through desert towns, dodging bullets, and shooting Iraqi soldiers. Therapists can alter the chaos of the experience by cranking up stressors like grenades and bomb blasts or adding scents such as sweat and gun smoke. Virtual Iraq has had a higher success rate than prolonged exposure therapy—previously considered the most effective treatment for PTSD—in which patients talk through their trauma in excessive detail. Virtual Iraq allows veterans to experience trauma the way they might relive an experience during a flashback. They are exposed to it again and again until the mind is able to assimilate and process the event. I wonder if Caleb has invented his own Virtual Iraq, his own traumatic repetition. Every time he sees a demon, he fights it. And like the controlled redemption of Virtual Iraq, patients cannot die or suffer wounds; Caleb always wins.

I mention Virtual Iraq to the neuropsychologist and ask if similar programs are being used to train soldiers to kill. I want to know if there's a relationship between post-traumatic stress disorder and the ways in which soldiers are trained to go to war. I imagine soldiers carrying these simulated environments with them onto the battlefield, overlaying Sadr City with the ruined corners of the

National Training Center's fake Iraqi city in Fort Irwin, now a fake Afghan city, where troops train in Hollywood-style counterinsurgency reenactments full of Arabic-speaking Iraqi-Americans, staged beheadings, goat meat.

The neuropsychologist says yes, scenario-based training is "let's pretend." There's noise coming from a house over here. The smell of burning tires. Simulated villages. Simulated riot situations. You might be in a course where you have your target and you have the civilians next to the target and you might miss and shoot the civilians. In modern warfare, technology means humans can pretend they're not killing humans. It's easier to kill someone when they look different than you. Words used instead of kill: knock, waste, take, grease, hose, zap, probe. Words used instead of person: Kraut, Jap, Reb, Yank, Dink, Slant, Slope, Skinny, Gook, Haji.

"But I've never met a soldier who thinks war is a game. I've never heard them say: we're going out on a raid and this is going to be fun. That's the kind of antics I see when there's no killing going on."

The amygdala is the fear organ—the fight-or-flight sensor in your brain.

Sometimes the amygdala enlarges, the hippocampus shrinks. Trauma can cause inflammation, atrophy, neuron death, and shrinkage. Parts of the brain can wither, rearrange, and die. The blast of an improvised explosive device can cause blood to swell, stretch, and break vessels. The biochemical reactions that precede trauma leave cells dead in their wake. The brain, unlike the gray matter we imagine it to be, can bleed.

The brain evolved from the inside out. The deepest part of the brain is similar to a reptilian brain. It's responsible for breath, heartbeat, basic survival. The middle layer, the limbic brain, evolved in the first mammals and has the ability to store memory. The outermost layer of the brain, the neocortex, controls the two lower brains and is responsible for morals, inhibition, imagination, abstract thought. Under severe stress, the center of the brain takes over. This part of the brain does not know how to form words.

"It's like this," the neuropsychologist says, "there was a bump in the road when Tom and Jack and Bill got blown up, so now I'm completely paranoid every time I see a bump in the road. I can't disassociate the memory from the emotion. It's replayed over and over again. Then you attach other scenarios to that danger zone. If you see someone that reminds you of Jack: emotion, old memory. People start attaching all sorts of scenarios to the trauma: any time someone gets angry with me, that means I remember that time Jack got blown up. Essentially it's an inability of a person to disrupt those memories. The brain is wired to help that person survive. PTSD is an uncontrollable memory wiring."

She says morphine helps. "If you inject someone with morphine after a traumatic event they won't remember the screaming of other people."

"What about a choking sensation?"

"That's probably more of a panic attack."

"What about his relief in deliverance?"

"It could be connected to the cult thing because it's a pretend scene, or pretend scenario, and because these people are really trying to bring out the dead."

With PTSD, traumatic memories as old as twenty-five years have been known to resurface with the strength of the original experience.

"A flashback is an amygdala memory," she says. "Don't go down that path because that's where the tiger lives."

He was marked for death. His whole life he believed something or someone has been trying to kill him. Seventeen years old and already three car crashes that killed everybody but him. When he was working as a grain truck driver doing 3 mph on an old country road, one tire dipped in a rut and sixteen tons of grain shifted. The truck flipped, rolled into a ravine, and onto the interstate. His head cracked on the glass. Consciousness returned slowly. Gasoline burned into small cuts on his face and lips. Worried he'd burn alive, he made his way out the passenger door, feet hitched to the steering wheel, rising from the cockpit into bright light. Fume-burned eyes saw the blur of the eighteen-wheeler, hauling ass.

The stories lived in his bloodstream, in the deepest cellular levels of his body, and he lived by them, as if by verse.

Again, another year, another highway, the rain coming down. An eerie feeling in his bones. The flashing lights of a downed truck up ahead and an eighteen-wheeler on his left. Boxed in. Raining so hard he couldn't see. Couldn't brake. A cold, swelling pressure grew in his spine. He felt fingers on his back. Someone was tapping him, trying to get him to turn around. He figured it was his heart. Then he remembered the taps he used to do with Kip in the *Evil Empire* when everything was too blurry, too dark, the machine noise too loud. A set of white teeth glistening there in the dark. *Kip, buddy, is that you?*

"Do you think the war has changed the way you remember your past?" I ask. "Or even, being here in Portal?" I tell him gently how sometimes when people convert to new religions they project their faith backward, using religion to explain difficult situations.

"That's all very interesting," Caleb says, "but I have no doubt that this thing has been after me my whole life. I know you think this all sounds crazy, and don't get me wrong, so do I."

He crosses his arms and presses his lips together like a beak.

"What exactly would be the point of me going through deliverance?" I ask. He keeps telling me to consider it.

"Let's say you did. What do you think you might have?"

I don't say anything. He continues for me.

"You're scared of the dark. What else? You identify the demon by pattern. Childhood. That's when these things first move in. Demons only inhabit the places you give them permission to inhabit. A dark experience you don't want to talk about. Could be something small. Would you be willing to share your trauma with me?"

"I don't have trauma like your trauma."

"Your trauma is just as important as my trauma. It's not more or less. If I cut off your arm, that's trauma. If I cut off your leg, that's trauma. It still hurts. In my book it might seem minute, but to you it's huge. It will be the thing that persuades you. Your weakness. For me it's failure and guilt. My father always said, 'Caleb, you're a fuckup. You're nothing but a goddamn failure.' And, you know what? I always believed him. It was a pattern. In every situation I was a failure and I felt terrible guilt. From letting my guys down in the chopper because I wasn't there to do anything about it, all the way back to when I had the chance to hit the home run and I let the old man down. For three weeks after deliverance, all I heard was, you're a failure. It was a test, but I got through it and it didn't bother me anymore."

"So it's just a change in your psychology?"

"Hmmmmpf," he says. "No."

"So there is psychology and then there are the demons. Can you distinguish them?"

"You can go through deliverance and call it whatever you want. In the classes I teach to soldiers, I don't call it demons. I call it quantum physics."

"Why?"

"Because demons freak people out."

The body of a deer shows itself in the field, grazing with a flickering tail, a bowed head. In the yard, at the edge of the light, two chickens and a rooster claw in the dirt, muddy from the cool places they slept in the day.

"You know, I prayed that no one would ever have to see what I saw in Afghanistan. I said, God, I'll go through as many years of this as you want me to go through if you promise me my brother and my son never go to war." He wipes his face with his sleeve. "Now my brother is a stone-faced killer and my son is trying to get FedEx'd to Iraq. His chin rises as if by an invisible string and he speaks his words toward heaven. "I'm leaving it up to you, God, that some big demon isn't going to come and crush my factory."

There's a kid in the field, walking around on all fours. The child pauses to look at me and then continue on, its bald head burning in the sun.

"Did you feel anything after deliverance?"

"White noise," he says. "All this white noise. I didn't even know it was there and suddenly it was gone."

He clears his throat. "Listen. I can't tell you to go through deliverance. No one can. You have to make that choice on your own. But I have an invitation for you."

The possession experience has deep roots in killing. Prehistoric hunters sought to be possessed by the predators of the animals they wished to kill. In the *Iliad*, Greek warriors became superior killers when the gods entered them. The Cúchulainn warrior of Irish mythology and the shock troops of the ancient Persian Empire performed possession rituals before battle. Berserkers, or ancient Norse warriors, undefeatable in combat, entered battle in a possessed state. They began with shivering, chattering teeth, chills down the spine, faces swelling with rage. They roared and howled to imitate the bear. Their frenzy grew. They bit shields. The edges of swords. They entered war with bloodlust, hacking and tearing to pieces everything they saw.

Lieutenant Colonel Dave Grossman, a former army Ranger, defines the first stage of killing as indecision, and the second stage—the stage of the killing itself—as enthusiasm. The origin of the word *possession* comes from the Greek word for enthusiasm, *eufousiasmz*, meaning "inspired by or possessed by God."

In Mozambique, since the civil war ended in 1992, it's assumed that when you return from war, you are possessed by the war; by dead enemies and dead friends. Your blood is contaminated. It can contaminate an entire community. The blood causes insanity. A ghost following a soldier home is a natural part of war.

It's easier to forgive a possessed soldier.

Upon homecoming, the soldier will be asked to reenact the killings. The ritual is called *kuguiya* and means "to stimulate a fight." Everyone in the village watches. If the soldier killed a child, he imagines killing the child again. If he raped a woman, he rapes her again. Only through repetition will the ghost leave.

If the reenactment fails, then the soldier is exorcised.

American society believes the same myth each election, that it is an exorcism of evil. We like simple solutions. In our foreign wars, we rid nations of evil. George W. Bush borrowed the vocabulary of religion for his war. Now Caleb borrows the vocabulary of war for his religion. Caleb sees the heroic, I see the tragedy. Not just because his friends died, but because of the way they're an emblem of our national tragedy. In primitive cultures if one is sick, it has to be a demon, and finding the one who cursed you is halfway to the cure. Does the exorcist too ever require an exorcism? People see PTSD as a problem specifically of war, but it's also a problem of our culture. A physical reaction is a sign of societal malaise. Their demons, and America's demons. For many, the military is not just a way to pay for college, it's also a way to save oneself from one's past, from the America you were born into.

PART IV

THE WAR ON TERROR
IN BIBLICAL TERMS

B obby says he was bullied in elementary school, middle school, and high school. He has a sweet, singsongy voice. He says nobody liked him.

Vivian, Bobby's wife, a woman with dreams of becoming a dancer, says she cannot dream any longer because her legs cripple and her heart beats too fast.

A man named Walter sits wide-legged on a chair. He's wearing snakeskin leather boots and a camo bandanna wrapped tightly around a mop of silky hair. He has a handlebar mustache. Walter doesn't want to talk about what he did in Vietnam.

A man with a greased pompadour and a turtleneck sweater steps shame-faced into the room. He has dark, shifty eyes. On his forehead deep lines curve like claw marks. He sits next to me. He smells of whiskey and baby powder. "I'm late," he whispers. "Call me Brother John." The Holy Spirit, as far as he knows, has never baptized Brother John. When someone put their hands on him for the baptism he saw dark, ugly faces on the back of his eyelids.

He's never known what that meant. "I think those ugly faces are me. I tried to see a picture of Christ and I could not. I only saw me. Ugly me."

Noah, a bearded man in a hoodie, wants to smooth over some marital issues he's having with his wife, Mary.

The professor has the voice of a man with a weak throat. He says his father once wrote the word *stupid* on a gingerbread cookie and gave it to him. He teaches literature at Georgia Southern.

A seventy-three-year-old man named Ezra says he's a pretty capable person but that he should have accomplished a great deal more in his life. He says that when he was five years old his pastor raped him. "I thought it was because the Father didn't love me." Ezra has been traveling around the country since he was fifteen seeking deliverance, getting different kinds of exorcisms. Nothing has worked. They told him his faith was weak. Ezra thinks it's because Jesus hates him. Ezra's mouth opens and closes. "I'm here and I'm alive. I think I'm barely sane. Sometimes I just think this is what life is about. That I'm just going to hang around and wait to die."

It's February, and snow falls for three days in Portal, hiding what people know of the land before it melts in a single day, sucked back into the earth. Outside, horses seek ways out of muddy fields, birds bathe in snowmelt, and grass has rotted flat. The continuous thaw of earth.

We are all at the Bible Covenant Institute in downtown Portal, a drab one-story building with a sun-faded roof. One side of the building borders Main Street. It's not a Bible institute but a local couple used to run a Bible college out of the building, and the name stuck. Now the Portal community uses it for different events, and the Mathers hold deliverance retreats here when it's available. Always Friday through Sunday. From one window you can see the Laniers' ING general store, where women wearing track pants smoke cigarettes and hold their faces to the sun.

Seven men and woman are here to receive deliverance. They've traveled from all over the country. Mostly Georgia, but also Maryland and Washington State. I didn't tell Caleb I was coming. I didn't want him to think he converted me.

Inside, rippled windows make the sky look like sloshed water. An elk head with marble eyes hangs openmouthed above a circle of red chairs. There are two rooms in the building. One in the back with its own entrance. A plain room with two couches and a sword hanging on the wall. The other room is large enough for a thirty-person square dance. Five foldout tables circle the main. In the corner of this room is a kitchen. They will feed us.

A team will exorcise us. There are generally five to eight people on a team. Each team has a leader. The leader decides on the demon. We will be exorcised in the corner, in a place the minister calls "the living room"—an area full of couches and foldout chairs and a coffee table, sectioned off by velour curtains hanging from plastic poles.

Katie isn't going to be on any teams. This means we're allowed to talk to her and tell her why we want deliverance. We aren't supposed to talk to the team members at all. We won't be delivered until tomorrow morning, and today, Friday, we will spend learning the basics of demons.

Katie tells us she had a demon called Jezebel. The slut demon, from the neighborhood boys who raped her as a child. The morning after her deliverance she ate eggs. "I'd never tasted eggs without demons," she says.

A very old lady raises her hand as slowly as a body rising from water. Her septuagenarian skin looks illuminated from the inside as if she continuously fed on lightbulbs. "I'm possessed by a demon," she says. Her glasses are big and reflective so no one knows what her eyes are doing. She talks about cabinets opening, plates shattering, heads spinning, voices appearing. Movie stuff.

I tell them that Caleb sent me and that he thinks the trauma of other veterans is going to transfer to me.

We break for lunch in the main room, where aproned women remove Saran Wrap from glass trays, chop potatoes, stack floury buns, drain pickles, soften aluminum-wrapped butter squares, peel plastic from single-sliced cheese, and stir iced tea in a blue cooler labeled with masking tape. A woman is cutting onions with a small blade. She is one of the team members who will be giving deliverance.

"I am the son of Jesus," she says.

The son of Jesus has on a sparkly pink shirt. She wears lipstick. Wide blond hair frames her face like wings.

"I'm the son of Jesus," she says again. Her hands rise simultaneously, palms up. Her eyes roll back. Only white shows.

The deliverees surround her, holding plates stacked high with meat.

"I don't get it," Mary says. She's wearing all red, shaking her hips, eating standing up. "Why are you the son of Jesus? You're not a man."

"Because," the son of Jesus says, and she pauses and her hands drop to the table in a loud slap, slides forward until her arms straighten and her breasts rest on the polished wood. "Because he told me. Because I know."

"No, I mean, you're a woman. Why the son of Jesus?"

"Man's the original. Woman came from man. When a man and a woman marry they become one flesh. Two individuals but one entity. We're all sons of God." When she speaks it looks like she's carving a clay statue really fast with her hands.

"I'm the son of Jesus. A disciple."

Bobby says, "Are gay demons more difficult to get out than other demons?" He is a small man wearing a big shirt.

"They aren't harder to get out but it might be harder for the victim to recover from the session. Usually, homosexual demons attach themselves to their victims during a moment of sexual abuse. Most don't realize this. They think there's something wrong with them."

"But it's just a demon?"

"*Just* a demon."

The son of Jesus touches me with her hand. It's cold like a wet paper towel. "I've never seen you before. Are you married?"

I tell her I have a boyfriend. She drags me to the fridge, away from the others, and gets really close to my face. It's covered in a thin patter of cream. "Any man who doesn't propose within a year isn't worth it." She waits until I say, *"Okay."*

Back at the table, they're talking about hormones and how they're getting in the water, causing fish and stuff to change sex.

I wander over to a couch and I sit with my legs pressed together, trying to finish my burger. A woman cuts my vision with her hand. "I'm Tanya," she says. We shake hands. Another woman says, "I'm Lynne." Lynne has short hair and green eyes like cut avocado. She has a peacock on her scarf.

"I'm in training," Tanya says. She holds her hand out as if waiting for a ring. Before I can shake, she pulls back and flips her hair with it. "I went through deliverance last summer and I just loved it. I came back to learn how to do it for the others." She leans forward. "Girl," she says, "get ready for wholeness."

Tanya had an accident but I don't know what happened. Half her face is paralyzed.

"Where do the demons go afterward?"

Tim told me that if the demons are sent in the wrong direction, they might run straight into an unknowing pedestrian, a grandma, a cat, they might even run into my laptop and destroy my hard drive. Once when he was still young and inexperienced, Tim sent a demon into the street and it entered a man—just this regular guy walking to the grocery store—and the demon made him shatter the window of his Mercury Mountaineer in the church parking lot. The demon stole his radio.

"I don't know where they go," she says. "Lynne, do you know?" Lynne shrugs.

Tanya grabs her purse, digs, finds a piece of Juicy Fruit, chews. The purse is a clutch sewn from the ass part of Levi's blue jeans. It has rhinestones and matches her jacket. "You'll have to ask Tim."

Paper plates pile up in the garbage cans. Conversation grows quiet. The kitchen door closes. Women clean. Children are ordered to play. The demon camp welcome lunch is over.

The minister begins his talk on demonology in the living room while Katie watches. A few of the men and women being trained in deliverance sit quietly among us. Tim says they might do this—watch us—because they need to feel things out before the exorcism. Tim has on khaki shorts, high white socks, whiter running shoes, and a Hawaiian shirt—the tropical storm kind. He raises his arms, and the tips of his fingers catch light.

He says we should listen to him but that he's not God. He says Christianese is church talk for the unenlightened. He says the first time he learned to control the weather his wife was holding on to a piece of sheet metal and the wind blew her in the air like a parasail. He commanded the wind to stop and it stopped. He tells a story about an endless bowl of spaghetti that's still somewhere out there in the world. He says people are trying to actively teach that there are no demons in America. He says once they were messed with by a demon named Jesus.

He's talking, rolling on the floor, rubbing his back against the wall, opening his hands near his cheeks and faking yelling. He's making us laugh. Throbbing. Red-faced. Screaming. We're sitting on the floor and in chairs and he is above us.

"The lowest order of demons are the foot soldiers," he says, "and in the Satanic Kingdom the most powerful demons rule over cities, states, countries. The demons assigned to warfare in the Western world use subtle tactics and attack ancillary measures in our life, trying to mess up schedules."

He demonstrates different ways people have come into the kingdom using the door as the metaphorical bridge between heaven and earth. He enters on his knees. He enters weeping. Indifferent. Screaming. He does it over and over again.

He says he hates Fridays because he's talking to all these demonized people.

"Just remember," he adds, "that if you go through deliverance too casually you're going to come out shell-shocked."

He leans over, lets his back bend and his arms carry weight. He walks forward and stands in the middle of the circle, a defeated gorilla. He rises straight again. He says demons know how to deal with Westerners. He says he can make our demon materialize if we needed evidence.

A simultaneous no, a begging, please don't!

Katie pulls a sweat cloth from her purse. She runs to him, makes the handoff, sprints back to her chair like those fast kids on the tennis court. Tim wipes his forehead and throws himself against the wall again. He shakes, letting his lips slack and glisten. "Does anyone have any questions?" he says.

"What're you going to do to us?" "Will it hurt?" "What is it like when the demon leaves?" "Will we know when it's gone?" "Will we feel it?"

Tim says he won't touch us. That it's not like *The Exorcist*, where people are puking and they have to stab you in the heart and your head is spinning and the devil is trying to have sex with you and your face is rotting. They vote on the demon—like a demon democracy—and the other demons follow. It's quiet. It just takes a minute.

He sits down and his hands make a beautiful curving movement to his thighs. He says some of the exorcists talk directly to God. Some see pictures. Some see scenes from movies. Caleb sees scenes from *Die Hard*.

"What if it's something you can't get rid of?"

"We've seen everything," he says.

I have a shopping demon! Lynne yells. I've got a divorce demon. I've got a retirement demon. I've got a debt demon. The minister laughs, stomps his feet.

I have an ice-cream demon, I say. No one laughs.

We take a snack break and eat peanuts. The minister eats a whole chicken in the garage.

"What kind of demon did you have?" I ask the saved man next to me. He's tan with white hair and a blue Hawaiian shirt. He used to play Halo on the weekend with the minister.

"Destroyer," he says. "Two heart attacks. Two lightning strikes. Nearly drowned under a tipped canoe. Car accident. Horse accident. And for five seconds, I was dead. I was having heart surgery and I saw it."

"How did you get it?"

"I was a Baptist," he says. "I'll tell you whatever you want tomorrow. We shouldn't even be talking." He runs away and I head to the bathroom but Tanya blocks me. "I saw half a dog in my room last night."

"You saw half a dog?"

"A dog means something."

"What demon did you have?"

"The fear demon. By the way, does anyone have any ibuprofen? My back hurts."

I dig around in my purse but the son of Jesus intercepts me: "Who needs ibuprofen when you have God?"

The son of Jesus prays over Tanya. They hear a pop. Tanya's back is okay.

"My back hurts too," I say for no particular reason.

They wave me over. They pray but nothing cracks. The son of Jesus asks the minister's ten-year-old granddaughter for help. The girl puts her hand on my stomach and looks into my eyes. She says my stomach is moving. She can see it moving. I feel her heat and it's the first time I'm scared of a little girl. They recite a prayer about lamb's blood and they rub imaginary lamb's blood all over my face.

Mary and Vivian, the wives of Bobby and Noah, are talking by the coffee machine. "I hate treadmills," Vivian says. "I'm a dancer at heart." Vivian jumps around when she speaks.

"I like walking, myself," Mary says, "because then I can talk to God. That's where I get my ideas."

"Ideas for what?" I say.

Mary makes a sound like air leaving a balloon and shifts her weight toward me. "I'm a prophetic painter. God shows me things. He shows me the river and the stagnant part of the water and says that's how he feels when I ignore him. He says that though the stagnant area is full of life, faith makes him all foamy and free and then he can spread the life all over the river."

While the women talk, an old lady with loose, blood-speckled rags on her feet starts coming toward me. "I love you," she whispers. Her cold hands wrap around my neck. She wears sport sandals. "I love you." I take her body in my arms. "I love you."

"Who are you?"

"I'm Brenda and I make the food." Her skin is blue almost all the way through, as if her veins had floated up to the surface and melted. She speaks in quick gulps.

"It's my heart," she says. "It works only one third of what it should."

"That's why you're here?"

"I don't want your pity. I get bronchitis terribly. I have thyroid problems. I have diabetes. I have nerve problems caused by the diabetes. My bad cholesterol is good but my good cholesterol is bad. And you know what? When I sleep, I stop breathing. Don't ask me how I got here. I do not know for certain. We did a lot of studying. Bible studying. Deep down Bible studying. But I didn't understand talking to God. You gotta understand poor Methodists don't tell you to talk to God, they tell you to talk to the ceiling."

Brenda is Portal born and raised. For ten years every Sunday, she walked two blocks to the Portal Methodist Church to hear the sermon of Myra Beer, who said there had to be more to God than what they were experiencing. Myra said the best way to find out was to go outside and look for it. So Brenda left and spent days at home waiting for God. One day she heard screaming from the streets. Downtown she found a red circus tent shaking with voices. She pushed through the crowd until she faced the traveling preacher with his handsome nose and said, I surrender all.

"Did I know what all that meant?" she says. "Nope. I hadn't gotten that far." She takes her sleeve and wipes a drip on her nose.

A group of teenagers passing through town, all wearing black, linger by the doors, peering inside, pointing fingers.

"Ain't they cute," Brenda says. "I hear they have sex in the school bathroom." She sucks her chin into her neck. "I told my son, 'I need to give you some sex education.' And he told me, 'Oh, Mama, you already did. You said don't sleep with any woman until you're married and when you're married your wife will teach you everything you need to know!' He's a good boy—straight from the

Lord, this one. After the Columbine shooting I went up to him and I said, 'Are you okay? What did you think about all that? What would you have done if you were there?' He told me, 'Mama, the Lord would either take care of me or take me home!' He's a good boy. You'd like him. Real good boy." A quick smile. Her throat is a long white curve. "The devil tried to kill him once," she adds. "Fell into a pond. Anyway, God told the Mathers to develop a college here and, well, them folks, they kinda do what God tells them to do—whether it makes sense or not."

There's a kid waving at us from across the street. We can see him through the windows. He's standing outside the ING general store.

"That kid," she says. "They found him in a ditch. His name is Beasley. He's a good kid."

The kid won't stop waving. He's moving his feet, bouncing, trying to raise his arms higher. With all the sun, I can't figure out how he sees us through the glass. I wonder if he's waving at his own reflection.

"What was he doing in a ditch?"

"Same as anybody you find in a ditch. I don't think he knew either."

A woman, maybe his mother, comes out of the store behind Beasley. She runs her fingers through his hair. He's shirtless and the skin on his stomach hangs over his pelvis like a skirt.

"Sweet boy, that Beasley. Sweet boy."

"What demon did you have?"

"One nasty big Jezebel. Nasty. They told me it was like a nasty toenail that had been cut but was still trying to hang on. I wish I could say deliverance was awesome—that it was the most fantastic thing I've ever done. But it was awful." She flaps her arms, beats her thighs. "I'm from the house of nasty! I used to get real mad at my husband because he'd be bossing me around. I was so mad sometimes I could eat nails. Sometimes I'd go home and I'd say, 'God, I hate him. I'll tell you right now. I'll be the first one to confess. I don't care. I hate him. What're you going to do about it?' God found the hurt spot and put his finger on it. I didn't get mad as much after that. You know, we've been married for thirty years. But this was before deliverance. God did a lot for me before deliverance. Now, deliverance. That was hard. That was really hard. One of the things they did was cut the generational curse line. That's how I knew I was from the house of nasty. Tim said I was."

I asked her to explain the house of nasty.

Brenda smiles and the corners of her eyes crumple like silk.

She looks off at a corner of the room. "I see demons. They're little black things that run around."

We gather again in the back room and the minister writes the word *enemy* on the board.

He says don't take any sass from the demons. He says they use the term *warfare* for a practical reason: people are dying. They're dying and slipping into eternal darkness. He steps into a square of sun and cups his hands in the light, almost like he can hold it and drink it.

"You're being stalked," he says. "The enemy's had six thousand years to practice. And let me tell you, he's good at his job."

Attacks begin as early as three days before deliverance. Sickness, car breakdowns, church uproars. One couple had been trying to come for five years. They've never made it.

Mary turns to her husband, Noah. "Were we attacked?"

Noah can't think of any attacks.

The old lady says her car broke down.

"Listen, don't focus on the war stories of the demonic guys. Just relax. If you don't, the demon will send you right out that door."

The minister hands out demon workbooks. A black plastic spiral holds photocopied pages. On the cover, images of bullet holes.

There's even a blank space to write down the name of your demon in case you forget. "Here," he says, tossing them our way. "A compilation of everything I've ever learned about demons. Who they are and the nature of them." Topics include Territorial Level Warfare, Primary Level Warfare, Kingdom of Darkness and the Realm of Demons, Carnal Christians, Prophecy 101, Demonology 101, Evidence for the Existence of Demons, The Punishment Crescendo (Sin Effect = X), Elementary Demonology, The Origins of Demons, The Nature of Demons.

The minister keeps a document on his desktop called "Demons I Have Met." It's a list of eighty names, but he's met at least four hundred demons.

Walter has a question. "Do demons speak English?"

The minister says they have their own demon language but they understand all earthly languages. "They're brilliant," he says.

The demons can be fear-based, anger-based, pleaser-based, martyr-based, sex-based.

"These aren't the names of the demons," he explains. "These are their functions. Their modus operandi. It's what the demons use to manipulate their victims."

The minister steps carefully back into the square of light, giving him a look of unearned holiness. "You'll know and understand your life in the completely different realm of angels and demons."

Brother John settles more deeply into the couch.

"What's the operational plan of a demon?" the minister asks.

Kill! Steal! Destroy!

"It's terrible. Don't think too much while you're here or you'll go crazy." That's why he calls it the living room experience. To calm people down. He's been known to give deliverance while eating a cookie. "I have to make jokes about everything because otherwise people will lose their minds."

• • •

The minister tells us these church people in New Jersey wanted to give an eight-year-old girl an exorcism and decided that the demon probably needed some outlet to leave her body. They drilled a hole in the back of her foot and locked her in the church basement for three days. The foot got infected and they had to amputate it.

Some ministers make you barf in a bag. Once a man choked his granddaughter to death trying to get the demons out while the mother danced naked and crazy. The police stopped her with a stunt gun. In Milwaukee a boy died because the pastor sat on him trying to get the demons out. In Africa, a pastor poured hot candle wax on the belly of a girl and then ripped it off with his teeth. Steel crucifix in the throat. Wood crucifix in the brain. A lethal potion of ammonia, vinegar, cayenne pepper, and oil. Wooden cheese board. Ceremonial walrus bone.

"A lot of you will want to see your demon manifest during deliverance. Trust me, you don't. Has anyone ever seen a demon?"

Three people raise their hands. Noah says they looked like wolves; Mary says her demon looked like a faceless man with a dark robe and funky hands; Vivian says she saw a short, squat demon that walked right up to her door.

"Like a midget demon?" the minister asks.

"They do seem to be getting shorter and fatter," she says.

The same three people raise their hands when Tim asks about our abilities to bring back the dead.

Mary tells us about the day she saw an ambulance come down the road and load up this young guy who'd died of a drug overdose and how she and the Christians surrounded the ambulance, put their hands flat on its side, and prayed until his heart came alive.

Tim takes his fingers and drags them across his face. "My ultimate task," he says, "is to bring a man back from the dead." He wants that man in the casket. Embalmed. Dead. That way there will be no swooning.

Ezra raises his hand and asks, "What is the extent of Satan's power?"

Katie opens the door. She shouts, "You've got thirty seconds because supper is on."

Ezra sits all alone at supper. He has old, thin hair. On the way to Portal he stopped at the International House of Prayer and had a calcium ball removed from his foot. "It was this big." He connects his thumb and index finger. "Usually it takes surgery to get these calcium balls removed, but not at IHOP."

Mary parades her prophetic paintings around the room.

"This is darkness," she says, pointing to the lower corner, where there are greens and blues and purples. "And this," she says, pointing to the yellow and orange section, "this is God."

"And these," I say. "What are these?"

"Those carry the breath of God."

At ten o'clock Tim leaves for home so that he may rest for his morning's work. Katie gathers us into the back room and assigns us all a time for deliverance. It takes thirty minutes and the exorcisms will be going on between eight and noon. Katie spreads herself on the floor. We join her, our bodies loose and exhausted.

We are marinating the demons, she says.

Singing begins and all the arms in the room rise together. Katie whispers to herself and to God. The whispers rise and meet the music of her daughter, who plays the piano and taps her feet. She is a thick, sensuous girl with dark long hair.

Candles burn and the light licks clavicles, hollows cheeks, carves eyes as if our bodies depended only on this light to exist.

I crawl over to where Katie is lying down and ask whether the demons know that they're about to get kicked out of our bodies.

"Demons aren't deaf," she says. "They can hear us speaking."

I ask what will happen if you aren't ready for deliverance but you do it anyway, and you don't believe.

"If you aren't ready," she says, "then a legion of ten thousand demons will come after you and they will try to destroy you."

She refers to Corinthians. "When unclean spirit comes out of a person it will go through dry places. But it will come back. It will see the place swept and garnished like a house but nobody will be living there, and so they will bring back seven worse with themselves. They always come back to check on you. It will come back with a friend." She rolls over to face me. "Legion," she says, "is a metaphor for the Roman legion. It's a Destroyer demon on steroids."

I rise from where I'm sitting and disappear out the door and into the woods and get in my car and run from them—the bodies on the floor. I drive out of Portal.

On the highway, the waffle houses glow like beehives in the night. I'm an hour out when Caleb calls. He demands to know why I left. I never told him I was going and he's upset. "Why didn't you tell me?" I tell myself that if I don't return and go through deliverance my leaving points to something like belief.

The psychologist Julian Jayne believes ancient humans were controlled by auditory hallucinations. If, let's say, an ancient human came across a tiger in the woods, she'd hear: run, fight, hunt. It was a hallucinated voice that mimicked the voice of the chief. Even after the chief died, the voice remained, the commands continued. In this way, the leader never died. He was always a ghost. Jayne believes this voice is the origin of human religious sensibility. A voice that became God.

On the way back to Portal, there's a severed deer leg in the road, in the middle of an intersection. All chewed up. No flesh except near the hoof, like a little red sock. I can't find the body. All I can think about is how it looks set there like a warning.

It's said that the first trauma, the original trauma, was the trauma of being hunted down by animals and being eaten.

I'm assigned to stay the night with a woman named Dotty, who lives behind the gas station. Everyone is given a place to stay for free with members of the ministry. Either that or they can choose to stay at a hotel. When Dotty picks me up that evening she doesn't want to talk to me because she thinks I have a demon. She stares at me with small, cloudy irises. She's an older lady with track pants and a blouse. I step inside her car and she drives across the street to her house. Fake plants and paintings of what look like interstellar nebular births clot the living room. On the wall a laminated sign of Uncle Sam says, "I Need You to Pray." In the guest room, the closed green curtains, bright with a streetlight, tinge the room with a sickly glow. The bed suffers beneath lace pillows.

That night I have a dream and in that dream they open my brain and they eat it.

In the morning Portal is full of damp, opossum-smelling air. The sky looks larger than the land, the palest blue. Saturday morning, and my deliverance is scheduled for noon.

I leave Dotty's house an hour early to walk around town. In twenty minutes I've seen everything. Lots of rusting lawn chairs in alleys, parking lots, and on rooftops. I find a dog in a cage large enough to house a person. The playground at the Portal Middle School is full of forklifts and deep holes. The main road crumbles on its edges and gives way to a gravelly dust.

The factory-sized red barn, a thrift store called Tumbleweed's, the abandoned Pig's BBQ, and Clyde's market where in 2008 a $275 million lottery ticket was won by an old man in work boots. "I don't have to work no more," he told the paper.

The town has two blue water towers, one bearing the town's

name in thick white letters, announcing that you are here, that you have arrived in Portal.

The son of Jesus hopes to turn Portal into a new Bethlehem. "There really is a Portal here," she said. And she had told me a story about how Tim was lying on the floor of the Bible Covenant Institute talking to God when the ceiling ripped open and he could see all the way through the sky and into heaven.

"Sometimes that happens," Katie explained. "He'll show up to town and he'll just rip a big hole in the sky."

Pepper Jack's serves collard greens and pork in buckets under incubating lights. A polluted stream runs parallel to the road from Pepper Jack's to the Bible Covenant Institute. While I'm walking, a van rumbles off the main road, turns onto the dirt one, and starts following me. He pulls to my side. A black man sticks his head out the window. There are two men in the front seat next to him. "You need a ride?" The van putters at the speed I walk. In the back, bodies move around plants and machines and dogs.

"We see you walking," he says.

"You're not from here," the driver says.

"We'd know if you was from here," the small man in the middle says. He leans forward and rests a hand on the dashboard. An ice cube moves from one side of his cheek to the other.

"Thirsty? We got Cokes in the back."

"I'm going up here to the church."

"We can drive you."

The driver takes his hat off and presses it to his heart.

Glory be to Jesus,
Who, in bitter pains,
Poured for me the lifeblood
From His sacred veins!

He closes his eyes, loses himself in the song, humming until the hum travels through his body and out his fingertips, and he shakes them with the violence of a pianist. The other men bow their heads. "Nice day, ma'am," the driver says.

They drive away. The van turns softly in the heat. They're gone. Disappeared behind the Bible Covenant Institute, where Walter and Brother John are being exorcised. Doors closed. Blinds shut. The locals don't know. I asked a man at the gas station if he knew about the exorcisms. He shook his head. "God's going on in there."

Down Mullet Row, a little alley of abandoned buildings running parallel to the Mather building, there's a reflection in one of the windows. A dark figure. I wait until the figure proves to be a man. It's the driver. Footsteps on quiet mud.

Inside the Bible Covenant Institute are soft piles of bodies. Just delivered, a few still waiting. The prophetic painter is passed out with a blanket over her head. Brother John is on the couch flipping through exorcism notes. I sink into the couch across from him. He leans forward. "You ready?" A rough laugh takes his torso to his knees.

Each time the minister comes in from the main room, his shadow moves like a tongue over our bodies, rousing us to step into the room where no one wants to go.

The minister enters and points to me. "Next victim."

There's a man engaged in a strange kind of war dance, putting his palms in the air, stretching his fingers wide, and moving them as if he were doing pull-ups. He's wearing a salmon pink button-up shirt. Burgundy hair sits high on his head. He has thick freckles like water spots. As he hums, his skin turns ocher and the freckles fade.

"Come on," he says with a growl, "come on. My name is Justin and I'm addicted to the Holy Spirit!" Justin cringes and shakes. He hits his head like a frat boy would when smashing a beer can to his head. "Y'all say it now! I'm addicted to the Holy Spirit!"

The minister leads me to a curtain in the back of the room. He parts the fabric. There are eight people sitting in a circle on foldout chairs. In the middle, there's a chair for me. A woman with long fake nails clacks its metal. The son of Jesus is there. So is the tan man who had the Destroyer, and Tanya, who saw half a dog in her room. There is also a ten-year-old girl on the team.

The team leader, as he calls himself, is the minister's son-in-law Kevin, married to his oldest daughter, Heather. "I'll be in charge of sending the demons away." Then there's the scribe. "I'll be taking notes. Someone has to be watching if the demons attack." Other than that, everyone is there to determine your demon.

For a few minutes, the team members talk among themselves. I don't really know what to do with my body so I just close my eyes and listen. "Is that a star you just drew on your notebook?" "No, my pen doesn't work." "An ink freeze or something." "Do you want me to get you another pen?" "Now my pen is frozen too." "Mine's not. Just for the record." "You're awesome." "It's these Uni-Balls." "I use gel pens myself." "I'm sweating over here." "This will be fun." "This should be boring," the tan man says. He lifts his hand in the air and lets it bend at the wrist. "Take a nap."

The team begins with worship. They tell God he is the greatest. Next, they secure the perimeter. The minister wants 360 degrees of protection around the building. Also, intercessors. These are men and women scattered across the country, serving as backup, praying and asking God for help. Twenty minutes are spent discussing backup and weapons.

"I'm a failing human being with no authority or opinion of my own," Kevin says. "No strength at all. We do not come in our name, we come in the name of Christ. We come again, Christ."

"Quiet, demons," his wife says. "Be still. Don't move or manifest."

A dusty radio releases a deep-throated voice: *Do not snatch your word of truth from my mouth, for I have put my hope in your laws.*

I have always obeyed your law, and forever I will walk about with freedom.

Everybody says they have no idea. They can't find the demon.

They blame me. The tan man says I need to let it out. "Show us your pain."

They start again. Nothing. No demon.

The prayers are repeated and again we wait.

And then it happens. That thing I can't see. Their hands seek places of rot. They start chanting. Their mouths twist to say *God*. Light collects in their eyes. One of them draws a picture of my heart in the air. They say my heart is half withered, like rotten fruit. They ask for Jesus blood, and the Jesus blood burns hot into my cheeks like a fever.

Everything is soft-looking and cries with the Holy Spirit.

I'm feeling blissed out. It's the term psychologists use to describe what converts feel following a conversion experience. The enthusiasm is usually temporary; fading the farther one strays from the organization and its followers. I walk out of the building and into the hot parking lot. There are a few women selling tickets to the chicken lunch at the ING Lanier's General Store. I'm tired enough that I can feel the distant flicker of dreams. My lids part, just enough. I return to Dotty's house, the one by the gas station, and fall asleep. They said this might happen. That sleep would be our strongest desire. I sleep, and in a muddled dream state I see a crucifix rise and then dissolve into the floor.

At dusk everyone is back inside the building. Creepy music plays like wind chimes. The team members keep saying that we look happier. They say our eyes look clearer, more stuck to the head. They say we no longer have dark circles or tired, purple bags. They're all smiling, a roomful of them, with smiles big enough to make their eyes disappear behind folds of skin.

"Your scales are gone," they keep saying. "Your scales are gone."

"Remember," the minister says, "this is about the warfare in your own mind."

Tim dares Brother John to get baptized and to see if those dark faces are still floating around in his eyelids. Brother John nods and Tim collapses into a chair, crossing his legs with his too-big black Wrangler jeans bunched over cowboy boots. He raises his arms and speaks. "Let's think of a demon speaking through a person, saying, 'You're a murderer,'" he says. "'Don't defend yourself.' You're not a murderer but you're a human and thus you're part of the human family. We all know that someone in this human family has killed someone. It's not the demons transferred through generations but the propensity to sin passed down through the generations that demons use to demonize. It's repenting the sins of the fathers. I guarantee that there's no terrible thing that a human being has not once done."

Some psychologists believe that the damages of violent histories can hibernate in the unconscious and will be transmitted to the next generation like an undetected disease. Violent histories can generate psychic deformations that can be passed on from generation to generation. It's the way that one's own trauma is tied up with the trauma of another. How the trauma of war can quietly trickle through our lives, possessing us, in a way, with the lives of others. Not just what we inherit from our parents and our family, but what we inherit from culture and from history.

In regard to the question of original sin, Kierkegaard wrote, "To the innocent man it never can occur to ask such a question, but the guilty man sins when he asks it; for with his aesthetic curiosity he would like to obscure the fact that he himself has brought guilt into the world, has himself lost innocence by guilt."

According to my mother, I was guilty in the womb.

Her first memory is of me rearranging myself to lessen her pain. She'd fallen in the woods and hurt her spine. I readjusted my body so that my fetal knee did not press into her shattered bones. Had an inheritance already begun?

When the Puritans accused Mercy Short of demonic possession in 1692 the minister Cotton Mather took on the role of Mercy's spiritual physician. He wrote down her nightmares in the book *Brand Pluck'd out of the Burning*. "There exhibited himself unto her a Devel having the figure of a Short and a Black man," wrote Cotton Mather. "He was a wretch no taller than an ordinary Walking-Staff; hee was not of a Negro, but of a Tawney, or an Indian colour; hee wore an high-crowned Hat, with strait Hair; and had one Cloven-Foot."

Cotton Mather believed Mercy's hysterical fits, and the Salem witch trials that followed, marked the beginning of Satan's assault on the New World. The Puritan settlers believed they were God's chosen people. The Devil was a good explanation for why they were losing the war.

Mercy Short was an orphan of the First and Second Indian Wars. The death rate doubled that of the Civil War and was seven times that of World War II. When Abenaki Indians invaded the frontier town of Salmon Falls, New Hampshire, in 1690 they broke into the home of fifteen-year-old Mercy Short and made her watch while they butchered her parents and three siblings. They dragged her north, on a wilderness march. On the way, the Indians decided to take a hatchet to five-year-old James Key's head. He'd cried for his parents. They chopped his body into pieces. Other crying children were bashed against trees.

Mercy Short remembered the trauma of her family's slaughter by pantomiming—in dreams, in visions—the torture of the Indians. In her visions the Devil thrust hot iron down her throat that ripped the skin off her tongue and lips. He engulfed her in flames. Blisters sprouted on her head. The room smelled like brimstone. Bloody pinpricks covered her body. Witch wounds. The

Devil made her sign contracts in blood. She suffered fainting spells, trances, blindness, deafness, muteness, anorexia, and physical contortions. Indian drumbeats filled her dreams.

If Caleb sustains one kind of hallucination, then America maintains another—the hallucination of a sterile war. If we consider the psychiatrist Jonathan Shay's understanding of PTSD, that it is among other things, the persistence of wartime behaviors into peacetime, I can't help but wonder if the United States as a nation is suffering from a form of cultural PTSD.

For Caleb, Katie says, it began in childhood when he was always trying to save one kid by beating another. Always saving his younger brother, John. Saving himself from the lies of women. Saving himself from the quiet failures of his parents. In the military he was always saving everybody else, saving their lives or making life easier. When he arrived in Portal, he was always trying to fix some company about half shut down, hoping to stop guys coming home from blowing their heads off. If someone broke down on the road, he'd have to pull over, watch them bleed, cover the wound. He was still trying to save his dead friends.

"Enough," Katie said. "You need to work for a living. You need an income for your wife. Your plans are too grand. There are too many veterans to save and you can't save all of them." She sat bowed on the living room couch, Caleb across from her. She had her long hair wound neatly in the back. "You can't be the savior of everybody, and, Caleb, you think you are the savior of everybody."

Caleb blamed the enemy for his ragged, strangled looks. Eyes swollen like a bird just hatched.

Katie prayed to save him.

The afternoon after he had the vision of the buffalo demon standing outside the trailer, Caleb went into the 160th offices at Hunter Army Airfield, hoping to talk to one of the commanders about the factory. One of the soldiers had an accidental discharge, and the guy Caleb was supposed to talk with, the commander, he couldn't talk, because he was involved in all the legalities of the situation.

Tim and Caleb had a meeting about what to do. Caleb owed twenty-eight grand in child support. Caleb borrowed money from willing banks but worries not much went to the children. Allyson, he's convinced, wasted it on her implants and gun collection. Still loving Cole Boy.

Caleb worked on the company with an Iraq vet named Roy, who went through deliverance but not with the Mathers. A different flavor, but the same thing. He went to jail for two years, lived in Statesboro, but sometimes Mexico. Caleb called him the other side of PTSD. A lot like Caleb but on the downside of everything. Living every day with it. Really down in the dumps. As far as seeing physical manifestations, Caleb doesn't know.

The minister blamed a new demon for Caleb's failure to save all the veterans from killing themselves. He dragged Caleb to the trailer for another session. They sat him down on a folding chair. The minister saw the demon move. It moved just a little. Something superimposed over Caleb. The minister said, *There you are.* Caleb told the minister that his bladder was expanding and that he was going to urinate on the floor. The minister thought the demon wanted Caleb out of the room to save its own existence.

The team found eighteen demons but these demons described one demon: the Ruling Level Demon of Antichrist. With an Antichrist the afflicted acts like a savior. It doesn't want you to succeed but it makes you believe you can. It wants you to think you're the savior of the world and burn out. In the end, you're not the savior.

The Antichrist leaped from Caleb's heart. It tried to rip open the mouth of the minister's son. The son couldn't breathe. There came up among his hair a horn, a little one, and in this horn were eyes like the eyes of a man, and a mouth speaking great things.

"Your idea of ministering to veterans," Katie told Caleb, "was birthed under the influence of the Antichrist."

In the winter of 2009, after his plans to help veterans failed, Caleb looked for contracting work in Afghanistan. A helicopter transport company hired him as an aircrew trainer, and he spent his days, back in the heat, hauling cargo across the desert.

But something was different. Flying over combat zones, he thought about Eden alone at home while he lay useless in the grave. He feared death. But death had never ever been a concern for Caleb, only an inevitability. He'd always had the sense he was drifting toward it. It was always around. If someone told him they were going on a suicide mission, Caleb would say, "Great, sign me up." Since the day the chopper crashed, he'd always packed a little extra ammo, a little extra food. Every time he stepped on a chopper, he figured he was going to crash and die.

Caleb called Katie from Afghanistan. "What's happened to me?"

"It's fear, Caleb. It's fear."

Afghanistan is where he hoped never to return. The open-air sewer at Kandahar Airfield shined like a coin.

Six months passed and the saving feeling returned.

First he decided to save his civilian crewmates, whom he feared would end up in the hands of the enemy, navigating blood-splattered terrain. What to do when the chopper goes down? What to do when the enemy arrives? As the flight crew trainer he offered to teach the civilian workers skills in survival, resistance, and escape. He organized a live-simulation training. Caleb remained vague in the pretraining brief.

During midflight simulation Caleb's voice cracked through the pilot's radio: *You're burning.* They were hit by a rocket-propelled grenade.

The workers fake-landed—they had never really taken off. They swarmed into the sun, arms waving. A few carried those who were labeled "injured." The burned guy. The guy with a missing arm. The unconscious guy.

The contractors carried the wounded over five hundred meters of plain earth. They gathered in a circle. They rested and thought it over, but they were wrong. Caleb hired a group of men from the Australian Air Force to kidnap them. The men appeared in the horizon's sunlit crack. Faces covered and weapons raised. The guy with no arm wasn't sure if this part was real or not.

Over time, Caleb started prayer groups in Afghanistan, men and women gathering at night, quiet explosions in the distance. Men hear things differently in the desert, they hear God differently. He began with the soldiers; the men he found stooped in the sand, the men whose wives had left them, the men who weren't home to see their daughters born, the men with bleeding gums and broken toes. These guys were grabbing him and saying, "I need to get ahold of that too." Probably four or five over there that were going to come back to Portal for deliverance. First Caleb would get to know the soldier, explore his wounds and secrets, and watch until he knew their demon. Then he'd bring him through deliverance.

This is Caleb at his most converted. It is better, he thinks. Better to kill the demons before homecoming even begins.

Caleb has a story about a thirty-five-year-old Afghan named Kaj, who circles an area near the compound day after day with a cart of goods to sell. Caleb wandered up to him and they got to talking. Caleb tried to negotiate with him, bribe him, see if he could make a deal so the Taliban would stop attacking the base. Kaj said he'd give Caleb what he wanted if he'd travel into to the mountains with him to help his father, a sick man with failing kidneys. The Taliban would never let his father leave the country to find medical care.

Caleb followed Kaj into the mountains. The father was a small man, sleeping in a dark room. His eyes hardly open.

"You don't believe in my God," Caleb said, but he spread his fingers flat over the man's heart and prayed, anyway.

Back in Portal, the son of Jesus moves around like a moth, disappearing into dark corners, pulling quiet people from shadows. She's in charge for the evening.

She walks over to a leather chair and sits hunched with her glasses on her nose, yelling that it's time to get started. No one listens. She waves the Bible.

I ask the tan man what we're doing. "The prophetic is like military intelligence," he says. "You don't want to fight the enemy without a little recon, do you?"

"Can I go home?"

"Go?" He shakes his head. "This is the best part."

Mary's on the floor making prophetic wet strokes with her fingers on an empty canvas with blue and red paint. She shows me her red fingers. "I brought an extra canvas if anyone wants to try." Vivian decides to try. She kneels beside Mary and forms her own image from drips.

"Someone pray," the son of Jesus says. Bobby lights candles with other candles.

"Someone pray," she says, louder this time. "All right, I'll start, then. I'm being awed," the son of Jesus cries. Yeah, yeah, she says, and then: yes, yes.

I look at the tan man and mouth the words "I want to go." He shakes his head.

The son of Jesus throws her head back. Yes. Yes. Yes. She rises. Her head seizures. It looks as if she's trying to shake ants out of her hair without using her arms. Her skin is blue near her wrists and near her face. She enters a fit, making quick, spastic movements like coughing. Everything is silent. There are only her words: *yes, yes, yes, yes*.

She walks in a circle, widening. Every few steps her head yanks to the floor as if being pulled by a string. She does it faster until she's pecking at the carpet like a chicken. Yes. Yes. Yes. She enjoys it. *Yes,* God.

The back door swings open and the air brings with it the smell of campfires burning somewhere far away. Two men step inside wearing big grins. They're called "the boys." The young-looking one with dark skin and wavy black hair comes to the center of the room and complains of nightmares.

The professor's wife points. "Bats flying around his head," she says with a gasp, and covers her mouth. She ducks when one comes too close.

With her eyes closed, her hands reaching, the son of Jesus feels for the invisible bats. "He isn't delivered," she says in a guttural voice, her mouth stretching.

"Say it louder," a voice commands.

"He's not delivered!"

What?

"He needs a really good dose of wine and oil. The blood and the oil just need to lather him up. I can't explain it. I think it's because there's dormant healing in his hands. His hands are cold. Wounds in his hands."

He gives them his hands, pokes at Christ wounds. "I volunteer at an insane asylum," he says. "They're getting to me. They're transferring. All day. I'm too weak. I see everything."

Everyone starts whispering, *Yes, yes, yes. Thank you, Father. No evil will become you.* I'm on the couch, slowly making my way toward the door.

They're rubbing his hair, moving their hands down his body, lathering.

"More, more," he begs.

"Your perfect love casts out fear."

Yes. Yes. Yes. Thank you, Father. Thank you, Father. His face scrunches. The voices of the insane leave him, draining onto the floor. He falls, curling, and then rises slowly again. *Thank you. Thank you.* They send him to the back of the room. Four people surround him and whisper about deliverance, using their hands to point to us, the delivered, the way we're all smiling. One by one.

"Who's next?" the son of Jesus says. She cranes her neck to look around the room.

Vivian runs to the chair and sits with her back stiff and her arms dangling loose at her sides. Everyone surrounds her, touching her feet, or touching her hands, or touching her hair. Her stomach. She's in the middle, showing us her neck.

Come. Come. Come. Come. The son of Jesus turns her head back and forth. Deep laughter from all. *Whoa. Whoa. Whoa.* Oh, yes, Jesus. *Come. Come. Come.*

Mary on her knees, wet-faced and whispering. She curls into a ball.

"Oh, Holy Spirit, yeah," the son of Jesus says. "Oh, boy, he just came in the room and is just waiting to rain down on us. If you want it say yes."

Yes!

"It's just misting down. Do you see it?" She raises her hands above her head and feels for the Holy Spirit.

Uh, wow.

"I'm feeling a lot of fire too," the son of Jesus says. "I think this means you must dance."

Vivian shakes her head. Her skin is covered in a thin wet film. "Not alone I won't. I can't. I can't."

"It doesn't need to look good," the son of Jesus says.

"But I would want it to look good."

"I want to see what Christ is giving you. Just let him live through you. Let him show you how to dance."

The son of Jesus reaches into the woman's chest and pulls out an invisible worm. She throws it on the ground.

I'm sitting on the couch. Slowly, I inch my way to the door.

Mary touches my back. "Are you okay?"

"Who has music?" the son of Jesus cries. Ezra dashes out to his car and returns with a CD. He holds it in the air. "Irish war music!"

We clap for Vivian in the thunderous Irish beat. Her arms move ribbonlike. She dances like an aerobics instructor, taking the left hand to her right foot, then the right hand to the left foot. Vivian spins. The son of Jesus taps her feet. The professor and his wife boogie in the corner. Bobby has a hula dance going on that makes the candlelight flicker.

The son of Jesus starts laughing. She says, *More. More. More. More.* Each time she says it slower, lets the sounds come out piecemeal, chopped up by laughter. More, Lord! More!

Vivian copies. The professor adds his own deep-throated "mores."

The son of Jesus begs and her laughter grows until she's screeching. The whole room follows suit. The sounds are like those of unidentified tropical birds. Vivian collapses. Silence. Ezra is next.

"I see warriors," the professor says. He puts his hands on Ezra's head, holding it firmly and gently as if it were an egg. Ezra's eyes roll. "I see a tribe before they go to battle. They're making noises with their instruments. There's the very loud consuming sound of war. Here's a new sword, Ezra. Put your hands out and go to battle."

Ezra parts his lips. He gazes at the sword and carefully retrieves it. He slices the air, cutting wide circles above his head. "War!" he cries. "War!"

Ezra runs back to his seat, still pretending to hold the sword.

Mary pushes me into the center of the room. "You go next."

"I don't want to."

"Come on."

Everyone is nodding. She brings me to the chair and I'm surrounded on all sides. The son of Jesus sits next to me and puts her face close to mine. "How's it going?" she asks through clenched teeth.

She crosses and uncrosses her legs, piles both hands on her knee. Everyone is summoned. Faces come close and then move suddenly away.

"You're one of God's favorite daughters," she says.

"It's true," they repeat. "You're God's favorite daughter."

God's favorite.

All mouths are moving. The tan man hums in the corner with his head down.

"No, really," the son of Jesus says. "You just don't get it. You're one of God's favorites. Okay. She isn't hearing us. The words are just bouncing off. I see a shield in front of you. Push that shield away." I push the shield into the son of Jesus and she gets mad.

"Oh, boy," she says. "You're having a hard time believing this, aren't you. The rest of us should be jealous. He's flipping nuts about you. He'll be the absolute love of your life."

Love of your life, they repeat.

"Oh, boy, oh, Lord. You'll never believe this. Look who just walked in the door," the son of Jesus says. "A pink mist. That means love is coming in the room. He wants to pour his love on you. Let him woo you. Jesus is going to be your greatest romance."

Your greatest romance.

Everyone hums and closes their eyes while having their imagined love affairs.

Noah touches my hand. He's crouched on the floor, looking up at me. "I see you in a hospital bed, lying down, and there's this golden liquid in one of those bags they put on the side. You know what God just told me? God told me you need a transfusion. I asked what kind. He said an identity transfusion. I really believe that God wants you to do a transfusion right now and that this gold liquid needs to pour in you and that you need to realize your identity."

Noah rolls over and disappears behind me.

"Okay, listen," the son of Jesus says. "You need to say 'I am lovable.'"

"I don't want to."

"Say it."

"I am lovable?"

"You're asking a question. Don't ask a question, just say it."

"I am lovable."

"You're asking a question."

"Say it."

"I am lovable."

"Say it. Again."

I say it again and again until I'm screaming it.

"You're still not saying it!"

I'm crying and bent over and they're all screaming at me to scream and so I just keep screaming. I hear breathing. I think I hear the bones in my neck crack. The son of Jesus is coming at me slow, wide, and ethereal in her dress.

Say it.

Katie enters the room and recites the Bible in a whispery voice:

"When the unclean spirit is gone out of a man, he walketh through dry places, seeking rest; and finding none, he saith, I will return unto my house whence I came out. And when he cometh, he findeth it swept and garnished. Then goeth he, and taketh to him seven other spirits more wicked than himself; and they enter in, and dwell there: and the last state of that man is worse than the first and that is how it will be with this wicked generation."

"You're in the enemy's camp now," she says. "All alone."

PART V

I AM THE VOICE
IN THE NIGHT

April Somdahl's trailer sits at the end of a wide dirt track near a patch of hundred-year-old North Carolina woods: a dark wall of yellow birch, flowering dogwood, witch hazel, wild strawberries, and the thick rise of spruce. Chickens nap in its shady border, burgundy heaps of damp feathers. A fence holds back the growth.

April didn't want to move to the trailer but her brother Brian returned from the war convinced that the Iraqis were going to invade America. He told April to move to the woods, to a place away from people, with enough land to grow vegetables and raise chickens. April didn't think the Iraqis were going to invade America, but she loved her brother and so she bought the trailer, a place where she could take care of him until he'd recovered from the war. Three days after she bought the trailer, Brian shot himself. They found him facedown in the Cumberland Center Pavilion, head blown off, bleeding on the steps where he married his wife three years earlier.

April says to get to the trailer you go past the hog farm, and past the dumpy trailer park, past the place where civilization ends, and then take a right at the balloon.

The driveway's a half mile long. No visible neighbors besides a small mobile home where an older man lives with his mother. There's six grand worth of oil stored in his shack. April says it's a country that takes no joy in the toughness of women. Men drive trucks but women don't. April bought a Chevy Silverado. Pissing everybody off.

In the end April bought the trailer for Brian, not because she believed his theories about the Iraqi invasion of American soil, but because she knew he'd need to be alone to recover from Iraq.

When I arrive two horned goats in a wire cage take their hooves to the metal. The trailer door's open and the television flickers blue. I walk up the steps. A fake Uzi in the shoe rack points toward a framed diploma from the Hypnotraining Institute of Northern California: "April Somdahl is hereby awarded a diploma as Master Hypnotist."

No one's inside. The air is quiet.

April and her daughter Khaia appear wordlessly from the backyard. In Khaia's arms—an oily black chicken, motionless and gripped by the child's tight fingers as if taxidermied into a position of grief.

"This is my blind chicken," she says. It's got no eyes, just a beak. "Oh, chicken," she says, rubbing her cheek against its small head. April and her daughter have curly black hair that sticks out nearly a foot from their heads. "Come here, chicken." Khaia loops a rubber band over the chicken's neck, slides it over the beak, drags it up the head until tiny feathers rise straight. "There they are." Two eyes like swollen ticks. "Not *really* blind."

The chicken is carried up the porch steps, into the trailer, set on the carpet like a child. Khaia disappears. The chicken paces around three cats wrapped like dolls in blankets. Another whacks at ribbon. On the windowsill is a caterpillar named Wormy who lives in a plastic home. Outside, in the backyard, April built a purple chicken coop. Beyond that, rumors of bear.

April's already making sweet tea and tells me she wants to sunbathe while we talk because there's a competition going on at work: she needs to outsexy Donna. "She wore this black silk halter top with these itty-bitty jeans and black heels that looked like they should be onstage. I show up for work in my sweatpants. 'Oh, I won,' Donna said. 'I look hotter than you today.' I feel honored that there's this beautiful person competing with me. She doesn't even know that she's beautiful."

April owns a tattoo parlor with an alien-war theme outside the Marine Corps base of Camp Lejeune in Jacksonville. If you go past the alien landing diorama you'll find a statue of a uniformed skeleton on a long march. As the war approached, the marines wanted eagles and United States flags. When the war began, the marines wanted meat tags to help identify their dead bodies. After the troop surge, marines wanted tattoos of their dead friends. Recently, the employees put up a life-sized dartboard of Osama bin Laden.

April walks onto the porch in her American flag bikini, muscled as a seal, sitting with her legs straight and spread, brushing her hair.

"Egyptian," she says. "Some will recognize. They'll say, 'You got African in you? I can tell by your cheeks. I can tell by your lips. I can tell by your hair, ma'am, with that curl in it. You got African in you?'"

April has Egyptian blood. The only reason she knows is because Brian wanted a genetics test. The guys in his unit started calling him an Iraqi: "You look so much like an Iraqi I hope I don't accidentally shoot you."

Brian knew they were right. One of them looked like he could be his brother. "Don't worry," April said. "I'll go ahead and get my genetics tested and let you know whether we're Iraqis." The more April thought about it, the more she worried it was true. She waited until a year after his death. Turns out they weren't Iraqi.

"Immigrant is what Native Americans call white people," Khaia says.

"That's right, fish lips," April says. April weeps into the hand towel and wrings out her tears on the porch and they evaporate into the sun. "I'm going to have to get another towel. I'll get one for you too."

Then I'm alone with Khaia, who's pointing to the cat named Pit Pat. "I think he died."

"He's not dead," I say. "He's asleep."

"I think he's dead."

"He's not."

"He speaks human. Years of talking to him makes him know."

Brian enlisted after 9/11, and it was less for the war and more for his father—to earn his love. But when he showed up to the recruitment office, the army told Brian he was overweight and the Marine Corps said the same thing. He dropped pounds quickly. His sister April asked how he lost so much weight. He said, it's easy—you just quit eating.

"Your dad is a coldhearted fucking old-fashioned marine," April said. "You're never going to get love out of him, so quit trying."

He was the type of father who would check the dishes for water spots. When he found one on the spoon in the silverware drawer, what he'd do is he'd rip the drawer out, dump the clattering utensils, then take all the dishes in the kitchen—breaking and slamming and piling them in a mountain of fucking dishes. He'd tell April to clean them all up again. She do it too—stay up until two or three in the morning doing the dishes.

They'd been living in military housing at Camp Lejeune. At

wit's end, April told her mother, "It's either him or me. I'll run away. I've got friends."

April ran away. Their mother finally took everyone to a bullet-shaped trailer in Kinston, North Carolina, on a street called Blue Creek Road. Their mother stayed in her room most of the time and smoked cigarettes and cried a lot. A year passed and their mother left them, five teenagers, alone, in the trailer. Brian found an envelope of cash on the bed. A handwritten note, too. April said she wanted to read it. She thought maybe their mother left because the house wasn't clean enough. Maybe they were arguing too much? Brian read the letter and then told April she couldn't read it. She never did.

April's biological father was in a freak accident that damaged his brain and so he couldn't help them.

They divided up household tasks. Brian had to take out the laundry and keep his bathroom clean. Nothing too hard. Sarah got a job at Taco Bell and brought tacos home. James worked at Golden Dragon Chinese Takeout and brought noodles home. April used her babysitting money to buy toilet paper. She didn't have friends with cars like they did. Sarah's boyfriend had a car. James had a beat-up old truck. When April met a boy named Dane with long blond hair, she remembered liking him because he had a truck. She met him in the month of April and she remembers that detail because her birthday was coming up and she saw him on the street and she said, "I'm gonna be sixteen, come to my birthday." He was a tall Scandinavian-looking man. It wasn't much of a birthday. Dane came, though, and they had cake and they have not been apart since.

One day Brian was eating his after-school snack in the kitchen and April was in the back room doing homework when she heard the front door slam shut. April ran outside to find that Brian's father had returned. He was barking orders, demanding that Brian get his shit and get in the car.

April said he'd have to take her with him. "You don't even know what kind of snacks to make him."

"I can only afford one kid right now," he said, and they left.

All those years Brian slept in a hallway. Eventually he made enough money selling pot to buy a beat-up car and come back to April. "I'm so happy now," he said. "I'm so happy."

When Brian shipped off to Iraq as a helicopter mechanic with Fort Campbell's 96th Aviation Support Battalion, the two made a habit of talking every night using Internet voice chat.

Nighttime in Baghdad, morning in North Carolina. April hooked up a mic and kept his spirits high ever since he saw troops outside his window, walking up and down oil pipes, and suspected a different reason for the war. April asked how things were going and he'd say things were fine. He lied to her for a while.

The first story he told was about the day he tried to help a wounded soldier whose cheek had been ripped off by shrapnel and all the flesh was just dangling there by a thread. He smoothed it back on the bone, gently, like papier-mâché.

Then there was another story about a ripped-up face. One time when he waved to a soldier walking casually across the tarmac, the soldier turned around and half his face was gone too. Brian marveled at the whiteness of bone.

But April said killing the Iraqi man is what really messed up her brother. There was so much blood on the windshield he couldn't even see the body.

April asked if the Iraqi man had a wife and kids and then she apologized for even asking.

Brian went on these patrols where they'd blast through a wall and they'd be shooting men, women, children, and dogs. On the other side of the wall was a soccer field where the Iraqi children played.

"Fucking shoot everything that moves!" That's what the soldiers told him, and so he shot everything that moved. "Even the dogs!" Brian said.

Later they turned the soccer field into a cemetery.

It wasn't too long before Brian invited other soldiers into the room at night to listen to April's voice. Soon the room was piled with soldiers from the 96th Aviation Regiment, all in their sleeping bags like on a grade-school sleepover.

"Keep talking, April," they said. "Just keep talking." If someone walked by, a guard, or a superior, someone who'd get the men in trouble, April pretended to be a radio and recited the news of the world. Sometimes she sang songs from *American Idol,* or lullabies from childhood.

But Brian always made April talk to the other soldiers first. "These guys need you more than I do," he said. Most all of them had PTSD.

The first time Brian put a soldier on the line, April said, "How's it going?"

"We need to exterminate out here!" the soldier said. "We need to exterminate all the cockroaches."

A few soldiers giggled. "Yeah, man, all these cockroaches. All breeding and taking up my air."

Another soldier's voice: "Yeah, their families all live in one house. They all live together like a cockroach nest."

April asked Brian why he wasn't saying anything. Brian said he was too worried about how much he looked like an Iraqi.

April told the soldier he was a racist and that all the Iraqis have mothers and fathers just like he did. After a long quiet, the soldier cried. "It wasn't me," he said. "It was them. They told us to think about the Iraqis like cockroaches because otherwise we wouldn't be able to shoot them."

• • •

Brian said he was happy in Iraq on two occasions. The first was on May 1, 2003, when April was home watching the news of President George W. Bush on the USS *Abraham Lincoln* aircraft carrier with the big sign behind him that read MISSION ACCOMPLISHED. "You'll never guess what," she said, "the war is over! Yeah, I'm watching it right now."

Brian called the soldiers into his room. April asked what they were looking forward to most when they got home. One guy said BBQ chips. Another said sleeping. Another said pillows.

Then the soldiers started thanking April for her voice. They said they were never going to forget their conversations. When they got home they were going to get together and have a cookout. They were talking and laughing, and then a soldier said, "But, April, it doesn't feel like the war is over."

"Well, maybe they just haven't told us yet?" said another soldier.

"Well, if the president announced it," Brian said, "it must be true."

"If Bush says it's over," April said, "it's gotta be over, guys."

"I don't know," the soldier said, "it doesn't seem over."

"I'm watching it on CNN right now."

"April," Brian said, "if the war is over, then why are we still here?"

The second happy moment involved a chicken, and Brian said it was the best day he'd had in Iraq. The soldiers, sick of the mess hall food—the soggy broccoli, warm fruit in a styrofoam cup, the burgers and hot dogs—decided to go to the market in Baghdad. They weren't supposed to be out, but they went anyway. They were ducking behind grain sacks and goats until Brian located a fat orange chicken. April didn't understand the economics of the exchange, but all that matters, she told me, is they got the chicken. They crawled back, maneuvered around stalls and cars, disappeared into crowds of people. When a military Humvee passed, Brian ducked. "If we hide," his buddy said, dragging Brian from his crouched position, "they're going to think we're fucking Al Qaeda and shoot us."

The soldiers made it back, and they went into Brian's room and they shut the door and they put the chicken on the table. They were just sitting there in the barracks with this chicken and none of the boys knew what to do. They didn't have anything to make that chicken a meal.

"We're going to have to go on *another* mission," Brian said. "We've got to break into the mess hall and get some spices and steal some shit."

One soldier kept lookout while Brian and the others went to snoop. They smuggled barbecue sauce, seasoning, a bottle of mustard, a spatula, and they took it outside and they cooked this chicken in the sun on an old grill. Other soldiers followed the smell and joined them with sticky red mouths, glistening fingers. The soldiers kept coming, and the pieces were cut smaller and smaller so that every soldier could have a bite.

"Wouldn't it be crazy," a soldier said, "if the Iraqis shoved a bomb in this chicken and we all died."

April remembered the day Brian called to tell her that he believed he was a vampire. She asked why. He said all his friends were dying but he wasn't dead. So he must be immortal. Immortal like a vampire.

"You'd tell me, wouldn't you, April, if I were a vampire?"

"You aren't a vampire, Brian."

"Maybe long ago vampires actually existed and I got their DNA passed down from generations and it's just our society that doesn't think they exist."

"I was there when you were born. I raised you. I fed you baby food. I would know. Of anybody, I would know if you were a vampire."

Brian took longer to respond to this thought. "I'll consider that. And you consider that vampires aren't born as vampires. They're made vampires."

"Vampires are just a myth."

"But, April," he said, "don't all made-up stories have some truth in them?"

In the month of November, the same month twenty-four women and kids were shot at close range by American marines at a massacre in Haditha, a retribution, the media theorized, for the death of a young lance corporal blown to pieces by an IED, Brian took a fork to the shoulder of a fellow soldier and then slumped into the fetal position. The soldiers in Brian's unit picked him up and carried him to a phone. They dialed April and held the phone to his ear.

April asked why he stabbed a man.

Brian said he wanted the man to fight him and kill him so then he would know he wasn't immortal like a vampire.

"You're going to get a punishment," April said, "but maybe they'll let you come home."

The commanding officer grabbed the phone and said, "Is this the sister that keeps my men locked up at all hours of the night? Is this the sister that my men miss meals to talk to?"

Brian was discharged, flew home in January 2007. He asked April, "Do you still love me?"

"I still love you but I don't know what's going to happen to you now."

Brian wanted to go back to Iraq.

"Why would you freak out so bad that you think you're immortal and you claim you're a vampire and then you stab this guy and then you still want to go back? I don't get it."

"April, my boys are out there."

"Your boys?"

"Yeah, my men."

April took Brian to the VA. "Don't lie to them," she warned. "Tell them everything you're thinking." Brian told the doctor everything he was thinking.

Do you feel like harming yourself or others?

"I will harm myself and, if someone gets in my way, I will harm them too."

Brian bragged that the doctor talked to him twenty minutes longer than he talked to the others.

It was the winter of 2007 when Brian started speaking to angels and receiving prophecies from God.

He called April his "little treasure box of secrets." *Open up, April, and I'll put all my treasures in your head.* Visions about the fourteen acres in North Carolina where no Iraqis would find them. Visions about his own death. Visions about Khaia getting run over by a car.

In Brian's vision of Khaia, she crossed the road and walked a mile to the neighbor's house where a woman lived with five diapered children. Khaia played, grew bored, and returned. The gate was locked so she tried the secret passageway under the bridge. It was flooded. She couldn't crawl through. Next she tried the barbed-wire fence but it pricked her. She tried the gate again but it was locked. Khaia got the idea that she would check the mail in the mailbox across the street. That's when the white car appeared, ran her over. Killed her. Brian was waiting in the trees to collect her soul.

Khaia didn't want to go yet. She needed to say good-bye to her mother.

They walked to April, who was on the couch weeping, and Brian repeated, "I'm so sorry. I'm so sorry."

"Mommy, I'm here."

April was too upset to see her daughter's ghost.

"We have to go now, Khaia," Brian said, "but you can come back and visit Mommy when she's calmed down."

Brian had visions of Khaia's funeral and the pink flowers. April walking down the street to find her little girl's glasses. She'd take those glasses and carry them for the rest of her life.

Brian talked about his own death as if it had already happened. "It all makes perfect sense now," Brian told April. "I know what I have to do. I have to die. I have to leave the physical realm and leave earth and go up in heaven and be part of the Army of God."

"Why, Brian? Why do you have to do that?"

"I've got to stop this war and save my guys. And the best way I can do that is to do it up in heaven. I'm going to meet the angels at the Cumberland Park. I'm going to put my hands out and they're going to walk me out of this body. The angels explained that I have to have a cause of death. So you see, it will only look like I shot myself. Really, I won't feel a thing."

A vision of April bent over his corpse, in a casket, partially decapitated, and her running hysterically out of the funeral home.

"You're not going to end up in a casket," April said.

"I'll come visit you when I'm a ghost," he said. "You'll know because I'll smell like musky cologne, like Old Spice."

April is allergic to cologne. "It gives me a headache. How about peppermint candy cane?"

They agreed and Brian said he'd return on the Fourth of July.

April finds a framed photograph of Brian cooking his barbecued chicken in Iraq. She sets it on the counter and says, "I hope you like chicken because we're having chicken for dinner." Her pale hands pull lucent breasts from green styrofoam. "I never freeze my meat. I like it fresh."

A teenage boy appears from the back room, looks at me, and turns around.

"How many kids do you have?" I say.

"Oh, that's my son. My third child was born still. That counts, though. I got four kids. I went through it all, so it still counts. It does." Her eldest daughter, Emily, has her stomach pressed to the taupe carpet, face lit by the computer screen. She carries with her the smell of electronics burning too long.

"What are you doing on that computer all the time?"

"Talking to my friends."

"Who're your friends? They live around here?"

"They don't live around here."

One of them lives in Europe but she can't say which country. She's never met any of them and she's known them in the virtual realm for five years.

"Why aren't you in school?"

"We're homeschooled," Khaia says. "Some girl kicked my sister."

"Some black girl punched me in the bathroom," Emily says.

Khaia chants, "Bad kitty. Bad kitty. Kitty, kitty, kitty. Hi kitty."

"I hope Brian is wrong that she's going to die next year. I'm so scared it's going to happen," April says. She wipes her eyes. She speaks with an unlit cigarette caught on her bottom lip. "Sometimes I get mad at him. He left me. I get so mad at him, you know, and then I'm like, man, that asshole, he probably just told me that my poor little girl is going to die just to fuck with my head!"

"Who was driving the car?"

"Brian said it was Khaia's daughter from a past life who asked God for permission to be the one with the privilege to kill her."

Khaia turns to me, her glasses bright with light. "Mama says I'm never moving out."

April sticks her head in the fridge. "Shit. We're out of butter." She moves aimlessly. Khaia rolls chicken parts in bread crumbs.

"Brian said she wouldn't feel a thing. She just got bumped a bit. I asked Brian, 'Where am I? If I know my kid's crossing the street

I will be out there to help.' He said, 'I know, April, but you will be too angry to leave. You'll see it happen. You will be right by the window when the car goes by but your brain won't process it. You will never remember that it happens because your brain will block it for you.'"

April has a knife in her hand. It hovers over a pile of chopped chicken glistening on a wooden board.

"If it weren't for my kids," April says, "and me trying to build holidays and memories for them, I wouldn't even celebrate the holidays. They're my chance to do life over. I'm creating childhood memories. I'm creating their childhood. That's what I've chosen to do with my life."

"Don't tell the chickens we're eating chicken," Khaia says.

"Once we had a chicken," April says, "who looked just like a box of KFC. His name was KFC."

Khaia leans over the counter. Her pink flowered shirt soaks warm sink water. "Mama was in the yard running around, saying, 'I'm gonna kill you, chicken.' He ran away. We never saw him again."

"Sometimes we hear him," April says. "He's out there still— high up in a tree, thinking we're gonna kill him."

Khaia points to the woods and she says, "We like to go out there with chain saws and look."

We get the machetes from the shack, put on boots and heavy packs, and take our legs high to press and pass the forest's soft-bodied vines. "Okay," Khaia says, "we just survived a plane crash. Got it?" She raises her knife high but it catches no sun. "This way," she says.

The machete is a dark bird fluttering ahead. The earth takes our feet, rises over them.

"KFC is out here, I know it. Did you hear what Mama said? She said, *We're gonna eat you, chicken*. He's been hiding out here.

Looks just like a box of KFC with legs." She stops in the brush, pulls a white mushroom from the ground. "Here, chicken, chicken, chicken."

The machete rises, finds itself in the skin of a tree. Khaia hacks and wiggles until the bark parts and the tree's white insides gape and its smell is released into the world. "So we know how to get back," she says.

The air is old, heavy, trapped there.

In the forest's center, a tree is felled and in its light we rest. Khaia takes her hand and lets it swim through the green light.

"He'll come," she says. And we wait.

Brian didn't return on the Fourth of July. No lingering smells of peppermint candy. April smelled cologne one time over by the couch but she couldn't be sure it was Brian.

When I find her spinning and stretching and doing yoga moves on the floor, she says she's training to dance for Brian.

"If I dance in a way that displays the suffering," she says, "then maybe he will understand. If he can see me, then maybe he can energetically pick up on the feeling."

When she dances she's kept company by a sound track Brian mailed from Iraq. She won't show me the dance. "I need to practice."

After Brian died, April drove his truck into the woods. First she drove it into a tree and then into a river. She got sand in the injectors. Sand in the fuel box. "How are you going to save me now, Brian? Look what you've done to me."

We drove to the places Brian drove. We searched for his ghost. The roads that wound through cotton fields, harvested for Walmart socks, which, on that night, absorbed the pinks and violets of the sky. We parked at a water tower Brian once climbed to see what existed beyond. What are they hiding up there? Brian had once asked April. What is the world hiding?

"The wanting of childhood," April called it.

Ten yards away, there's an old Coke machine and an abandoned shack. April tells me a story about the day Brian's truck broke down on this road and he slipped a quarter in the slot. A warm, dusty Coke rolled out. As ritual, each of us put a quarter in the slot.

"If a Coke comes out," Khaia says, "Brian's with us." Khaia pushes the button. She looks at me. She pushes again.

The day the police discovered Brian's body at the Cumberland Center Pavilion, April's mother called to tell her the news.

"Oh, Mom," April said, "it's okay. I just talked to him actually. I should go because he might be trying to call. I told him to call me in the morning."

"What time did you talk to him?"

April said around one in the morning. Her mother said they found the body around seven.

"April, we knew this was going to happen. I have the suicide note." She carried it around in her purse. She wouldn't let April read it.

"I didn't know," April said.

"You knew."

"I was talking him out of it."

"You knew."

"I did everything I could."

"You knew."

The night before, Brian called at twelve forty-six in the morning. April was already in bed with her husband, Dane. Ever since Brian left for Iraq she'd slept with her cell phone underneath her pillow. Just in case.

April said, "Hello?"

Brian said, "Good-bye."

April said, "Hello?"

Brian said, "April, I'm telling you good-bye. I knew you'd be mad if I didn't say good-bye. Good-bye, April. Good-bye. Good-bye. Good-bye."

April asked where he was going.

Brian wouldn't stop saying good-bye. He said it over and over again, dozens of good-byes. April remembers about thirty good-byes, all in different voices, as if he were saying good-byes for the others too.

April just sat there on the phone while the voices roared in her ear: Good-bye.

"Brian," April said. "Please stop."

"Good-bye," he said again. "Good-bye."

"Where you going?"

"Going away," he said. His wife was getting an abortion and the last reason for him to be here was gone. "You told me I would enjoy being a dad."

"She can't get an abortion because she's in her third trimester. Go to bed, baby boy. Sleep in your jeep. No one will bother you there. Call me in the morning."

That's when Brian shot himself.

"Hello? Brian, you dropped your phone." She waited. "Okay, I'll just wait a second."

181

Dane rolled over. "Is everything okay?"

April turned to him. "Brian's okay. He said he'd call me in the morning."

"Good-bye, Brian," April said. "Good-bye."

April chain-smokes in running shorts and a cotton tank, sometimes lighting a new cigarette before finishing the old. Her fingers spread on the window, making it wet with her heat. April puts her tongue in her cheek as if to store it there. A cat with a blue blanket over its head stares from the doorway like a tiny Mother Teresa.

Pit Pat licks my calves, sticks her butt in the air. "That means she likes you," April says.

We walk out onto the porch. The air is cool but the wood is warm with yesterday's sun. "I remembered that he said not to talk about the pact." She gathers her feet beneath her thighs. "I tried to bring it up a second time and he said he wasn't going to talk about the pact." She drags her eyes from her feet to my face. "Brian said there were a bunch of guys who'd get together and they were meeting in rooms in their houses and talking about all dying for a purpose. Brian boasted about how they had about six guys in Germany on board. He was excited about how many people he could get into the secret suicide group at Fort Campbell. I asked him, 'What are you doing? Are you starting this? Did you start this?' He said somebody over at Fort Campbell started it."

February. He died on the twentieth of February. That's when he told April. He said his friends were suffering because he was suffering. They were the ones who had to gather around him while he cried his eyes out. He put his buddy Chris on the phone. Chris was mad at April. She told Chris he wasn't doing the right thing by saying that if you commit suicide you should join some secret pact. "I wish I would have gotten along with him better. I think he was a different Chris from the one in Iraq."

Brian took the phone. April said, *some friends you have.* This upset him. He thought he had good friends because they told him that if he was going to die then they'd die with him. "We'll die together," he said. "One by one, until every bit of the war stopped and everyone was brought home."

April stretches, reaches all the way to her toes, and rubs them until they wiggle. "I remember he said they'd die staggered. They wouldn't all die at the same time, but that they would pick dates. That way no one would forget. That way everyone would always be remembering the war."

April thinks Brian was scheduled to die after Jeffrey Lucey, who died on the sixteenth of January. The twenty-three-year-old hanged himself with an electric cord six days after the VA put him on a wait list in St. Cloud Hospital in Minnesota.

April imitates the soldiers: *We should all do it together! Do it! Do it! Do it together!*

"But, you know," she says, "Brian recognized that he was traumatized. That he was damaged. Others recognized that they had some damage. That's why they decided to form this suicide pact. Which actually makes sense. Before Brian died he was incredibly calm. He was almost happy. That must be why."

Khaia sets a finger on her mother's leg. "Mama, you want a pear?" She cocks her head and holds the green fruit out to her mother, using two hands. "They're full of goodness."

April grips her daughter's hand. "I don't want a pear, honey." April pulls her legs to her chest and sucks on her cigarette.

"Do you want a pear?" she says to me. "They're full of goodness."

"Thank you," I say. "I'm okay."

April has theories about how a woman from the military tried to break into her computer system and steal recordings of the soldiers' voices. When the woman called, April kept repeating, "I did everything I could to stop him. I did everything I could to stop him."

"I can't put names to the voices," she says. "I wish I could find them."

April's body keeps unraveling. First she leans back, and then spreads her arms and then her legs.

"You know, I think he was afraid of dying. I don't think he was afraid of the stupid shit he was talking about. I don't think he was scared of fucking bombs landing on my fourteen acres or Iraqis coming in and slaughtering us. I think that might have been just a made-up fantasy along the way. A story to entertain me." April raises her head toward the sky and grips her hair. She swallows, holds in her words. "Oh, my God, it was, it was. He made it up. I just remembered a couple little words that he said right before he explained doomsday to me. He said, 'I don't care what you tell America, April. Tell America that I thought the world was going to blow up. Tell America I thought this and that.' He didn't really think that. If he did he would have phrased it in a way that showed that he was really thinking it. He wouldn't have said: 'Tell them the truth.'"

"Tell who?"

April releases her hair. "Whoever asked how he died in Iraq after he was gone."

"He didn't die in Iraq."

"He did," she says. "He killed himself here, but he died in Iraq."

A Harrier jet flying northeast from Camp Lejeune grows big in the distance, flying low over the house, showing its metaled stomach. We lay our bodies flat on the porch and let the vibrations run up through our skin and out our mouths.

"You know what the soldiers said at night? 'April, you've been great. Thank you for staying with us and being the voice in the night.'"

April rolls her head to me but it's too dark to see each other's faces.

She says, "I am the voice in the night."

• • •

After a week at April's, sleeping on her couch, hearing her stories, I drive out and stay at a hotel. The night desk clerk is a Pakistani woman asleep in an open window. "Excuse me." I touch her on the shoulder and she shakes to life.

"Fifty-five dollars."

I point to the sign. "Twenty-nine."

"That's if you stay for a week." She has banana in her cheeks. A plate of cut bananas at her side, browning on the edges. Their centers still bright.

"Does anyone stay for a week?"

She shakes her head and swallows.

Coke machine glow lights the cement hallways. When I go to my room, I set my things down and then walk outside. The sky is blue before black. A man is standing on the second-floor balcony, bathing in moonlight, wearing camo and combat boots and sucking a cigarette. I recognize him from Portal. It's Walter. I wonder if he's been staying here for weeks looking out at the middle distance. I say nothing. What to say?

I'm sorry you had Lucifer.

While I sleep, the polyester curtain thumps over the air conditioner, expanding and contracting like lungs. My eyes feel dug around in, sore to the touch. My mouth burns with dehydration. Sleep comes fast. The room darkens. My eyes open. In my dream there's a bat the size of a man standing in the corner of the room. He's the texture of an old date. With one pump of its wings he flies to me. Lands on me. Finger-sized claws explore my neck. I stay limp. It does its thing. Its warm, velveteen squeeze. The bat trembles.

In the book *The Secret Lives of Puppets*, Victoria Nelson writes a story about a woman at the peak of her depression. She's sitting at home one day, collapsed on the couch, when a giant black bird flies into the room. It is a demon, she knows. The bird speaks to her in a strange language. The woman recognizes that if she speaks back she will be *consorting with the gods*. She refuses and it's because of this refusal that the black bird flies away and she is at peace.

I think about this story when, months later, a bat—a *real* bat— flies into my room and sits on my neck. Caleb's stories linger like a contagion.

When a real bat comes into your room at night, it's advised, the doctors at Mercy Hospital in Iowa City say, that you receive a vaccination for rabies. When one enters the second stage of the rabies virus, it's called the furious stage and the body enters violent fits: the body arcs, the stomach lifts, the head falls back. The voice is *raucous* and *crowing*. Face twitching means you can't close your eyes. That means you have to watch your death.

Dim lights burn in every hall of the hospital. Prayers chant on repeat from loudspeakers. I brace myself before the swab's cold lick, the chemical burn, the cratering of deltoid skin at the injection point.

Months later. Another bat, circling my head, tangling in my hair. It's like their voices roaring again.

After the crash, in 2005, Caleb bought a brick engraved with the name Kip Jacoby. He set it among the hundreds of other bricks in the ground engraved with the names of dead soldiers.

On a night with no moon in 2010, Caleb drives to Savannah to be alone with his own memorial. It's the Blue Star Memorial in a park full of bearded cypress.

There's a loudspeaker that plays Lee Greenwald's "God Bless the USA" in the afternoons and a black granite wall divided up among memorializing images of America's foreign wars.

Caleb finds Kip's brick. He licks his hand and wipes saliva on Kip's name, darkening the words.

The trees moan and Caleb's lips move in the dark. "I'm back in the fucking desert, Kip." Caleb has a deep-sea-fish look about him. Eyes blue and glowing. He sits with his head hanging and his legs crossed. The light from Venus borders a small cloud.

"I don't know what to do, Kip. I'm tired of the war. I'm tired of Afghanistan. I'm not good at anything here. Everything I am good at is over there."

Caleb drapes his arms over his knees and lets his fingers stretch and feel the air.

"Some days I wake up and I'm not sure if I've moved forward at all in my life, Kip. It's the same family drama. The same war. The same fucking desert in Afghanistan."

Caleb, along with most of the other men in Portal who are part of the Mather group, work in Afghanistan. It's for this reason that, in a small wooden duplex tucked in a quiet neighborhood between Portal and Statesboro, the son of Jesus has a home she calls the House of Women. Everyone who lives there is waiting for their men to come home from the war.

She blames God for the move. "He has something in store for us." Her husband's in Afghanistan, and her eighteen-year-old son just joined the air force. She lives with Marianne, a church member, and her twenty-nine-year-old daughter Ruth. "You won't get to meet a lot of the men in our ministry," she says.

When I walk through their front door, the son of Jesus looks at me in a frightened way. I'd just returned from April's trailer. She keeps her distance. "You were staying with those people, weren't you?" I had told her at the deliverance retreat.

She folds her arms and glares at me in the way only a worried mother can—an equal amount of cruelty and kindness.

The son of Jesus paces. She lifts her hands in the air as if to feel my words. She takes them and puts them in her mouth.

"How long were you there?"

"Not long. A week."

"Tell me again," she says, and I tell her again about the bat dreams. I note that, when I'm trying to interview them, they try to make me the subject. Among these folks, she is the go-to person for dreams. She attends conferences, leads sessions, takes calls. "I want to take a look at you," she says, "but first we need to wait for Brett."

"Is that—?"

"He's just." She sets a finger to her lips. "He's just Brett. The others should be home soon."

Lamplight muddies the living room. There's a bookshelf stacked with Bibles. Only Bibles, and dozens of them. Hardwood floors gleam dark as water. Men wearing tool belts wander around the house, looking for ways to fix the heat. All the food in the pantry is on the floor, stacked high on the counter or on the kitchen table. The heating man is in the pantry on his hands and knees.

Ruth and Benjamin, her children, are on the couch in the living room playing video games. Benjamin rocks and jumps while he plays. He calls his sister Fuzzy.

"Fuzzy," he says. "Hey, Fuzzy. Guess who got drunk last night?"

Ruth won't have any of it. "Only thing you'll get drunk on is caffeine," she says.

"You've never had a sip in your life."

"I ate a bourbon ball, Fuzzy. I was wasted. Remember?"

The son of Jesus laughs and holds Benjamin's face. "I had a thought about *your* dream, Benjamin. We're going to write down your dream and put it in the mail and send it to our address. In case something happens. If something happens we're as innocent as possible, you hear?"

Benjamin embraces his mother. "I love you," he says. He has on Superman pajama pants.

"Take this paper," his mother says. "Go and sit and write down your dream. Tell me what you remember."

Ruth's phone goes off but she doesn't recognize the number. She sets it on the table and when the voice mail dings, she listens. "Shit shit," she says. "It was my dad." She's staring into her phone, pulling on her hair, repeating, "I missed it. I missed it."

She talks about holy wars and the Old Testament, the parts where Father would say to Israel: you need to go fight these people or you're not going to have peace and they'll come after you and you'll be influenced by their gods! "Every time Father told them to fight they were victorious. Do I believe Father is telling us to go to Afghanistan? I don't know. I think Afghanistan is a nation that needs to know God. Do I think it's the great evil? I don't know."

"Are you worried about your dad?"

"Over some of these Arab countries," she says, "there are large demonic beings and they tell their underlings to attack or to destroy. You hear about American civilians, contractors, relief aid workers being blown up on the side of the road. You probably saw the photos of the charred bodies hanging from the bridge." She touches her finger to her lip. "I hope they get to be at the same base."

"Do you think George Bush has a demon?"

"Well, anyone who strives to work on Capitol Hill is demonized. Without a shadow of a doubt, Hillary is Jezebel. No doubt. Bill's a total Ahab."

"I was outside," Benjamin interrupts, remembering his dream, "and there was a police officer in my room but it was like I was in the middle of the room. I saw its winter white walls. The officer— she said they found drugs. Specifically marijuana." He raises his finger in the air. "They said it was in a Wendy's bag."

"A female cop?"

"Yeah."

"Was she familiar to you?"

Benjamin presses his pencil eraser to his cheek. He shakes his head.

"I don't know what the future holds," the son of Jesus sings, "but I know who holds the future." She does a quick dance.

Benjamin scribbles his dream. "How do you spell the word *room?*"

"R-O-O-M," his mother says.

"Maybe God is saying fast food is crack," Ruth says, standing by the window, stretching her arms in dim porch light coming in through the screen.

"It's that or you need to take out the garbage in your life," the son of Jesus says. She looks at me, waves me into the kitchen. Tonight she's making something called the cheese ball for her coworkers.

"Let me tell you about my favorite dream," she says, pouring cheese-ball ingredients in a bowl. "I'm lying on a mattress on the floor and I have all these little pieces of blanket covering me and there's a Coke machine next to me and in walks this huge lion with these gorgeous blue eyes. He nudges me. He's the Lord. The Coke machine means that my relationship to him is going to be refreshing."

She takes a beater out of the cabinet and plugs it in and we listen to its roar. "There," she says, and she pulls out the beater and licks it. "Everyone just guzzles down this cheese ball. It's real simple—just cream cheese and onion and old-fashioned cheddar and butter."

She takes another lick.

"You want a beater?"

"I'm okay."

"I know you do."

"You're right," I say. I take the beater and lick.

The phone rings. The son of Jesus hurries to rinse her fingers before reaching for the phone. "Hello? Hello? Rats."

She leaves the kitchen and returns with a box of fudge. "I make the best fudge in the world," she says. "Want some?"

I take the fudge and I push it in my mouth. She touches my shoulder. "My kids are nine years apart," she says, bending over, searching the butcher-block shelves, stacking cookie tins in her arms. "Lemon bars," she says, opening a tin. "Try this."

I press a lemon bar in my mouth.

"Yeah," she says. "You know. I had all these miscarriages between the two of them. Let me tell you something." She leans against the sink. "I was crawling in bed one night and suddenly I was in heaven. I saw this cute little girl in a blue dress. I asked the Lord: Is that some part of me? Or is that me? What's going on? I was lost in heaven. This one is yours, the Lord said, and suddenly I was enveloped in heaven and I was meeting all my dead children. How many kids? I don't know. I was so depressed at the time. My body didn't have the progesterone to carry the babies past my periods. The doctors started giving me a progesterone depository but it wasn't strong enough. One baby I carried two months. One a little longer. One was born without a brain. The doctor looked at me and said that there was nothing he could do. But in heaven, they were so beautiful. They had never known sin. They had never known this earth. And when I was up there, suddenly, I was glad they were never born. One even remained an infant—just for me to hold. I said to the Lord, are they all here? Are all my children here? He said, Do you really think I would let one of yours fall?"

Ruth and Benjamin are still sitting on the couch in the family room facing the television, arguing over the remote. "My babies," she says. "Can I tell you something else? This might blow your mind. This was three years ago. The Lord took me into a vision. In front of me I saw a great wall of fire. I saw him walk into the fire and I knew I was to follow him. I followed him. I was standing in hell. I'm seeing a man on the floor in excruciating pain. He was retching and writhing in the most horrid amount of pain—just screaming. He was probably new to hell. He sits up a little and says: pray for the living, not the dead. Then I hear some woman yelling at me, *You are here to mock me. You are here to make fun of me.* She is screaming this at me. She is wild. And then the Lord shows me one more person—a young man standing there doing nothing. I made this choice, he says, I made this choice to be here. That's when I realize that everyone in hell had made a choice to be there. By their choices on earth, they chose hell."

"Who were they?"

"They were all from different eras. The young boy, he probably died somewhere between 1910 and 1930. The woman, she might have been in hell for two or three hundred years. The young man, it was like his feet were in rock and he was just standing there ripping away at the wall. I could hear other types of screams and moans coming from the dark. Since then, I don't challenge the Lord about it. I know that everyone who's in hell made the choice to be there. There's no denial in hell. I came out of that vision and it haunted me for a very long time."

"Did you see any demons?"

"No," she says, "I didn't see any demons. I only saw people."

When Marianne returns, she throws her purse on the table. "Don't tell anyone," she says. "I just got a promotion at Walmart." She's a large girl with an upturned nose, wide brown horse eyes, and shimmering, poreless skin. She never stops smiling.

"What's wrong with you?" she says.

Brett returns at midnight. He bursts in from the dark. I recognize him—the same boy who came to the Bible Covenant Institute the night of my deliverance. The boy who had bats flying around his head. The boy who worked at a mental institution. The boy who carried a Bible in his right pocket with a gold thread dangling low.

"She needs a second look," announces the son of Jesus, and Brett nods like it's no big deal. He's in town because there's a deliverance retreat in the morning. He drove to Portal from Tennessee, where he works a regular gig at the circus.

Everyone keeps looking at me. I don't want them to do whatever they are going to do, but I'm curious.

"This woman," Ruth says, panting slowly between words, "did she give you anything?"

"Just some ChapStick."

"The demons can hide. Talk to the ChapStick. Tell the ChapStick: you're just an object."

They're all staring at me, waiting, and so I tell the ChapStick that it's just an object.

"And remember," the son of Jesus says in a soft voice, "Jesus is going to woo you. I see a pink cloud coming into the room right now."

"That's what you said last time."

She puts her hand to her breast and grows quiet to search her memory. "He just won't give up on you, will he?"

To be polite I sit down among them, gathered on the carpeted living room floor, beneath the light of a single lamp. Their veined fingers climb the air. Voices humming.

"I see despair," says the son of Jesus.

"I see infinite sadness," says Marianne.

"Suicide," says Ruth.

Their heads bob.

I feel a burning in my spine. Something moving around. What I feel is this: my spine being pulled, whole and wet, like the long gut of a shrimp. It's not what I believe. It's my body betraying me.

"It's gone."

The son of Jesus says, "There it is. I see it. Over in the corner."

"Get out!" Everyone collapses to the floor.

I have my hands on my face, crying. There's no perfectly objective response. When trauma moves from one person to another, psychologists call it transference. It's the same word the Mathers use to describe the movement of demons.

"The suicide demon," the son of Jesus says, "is very focused. I've had it follow me home twice. I've had to battle it. One day I'm unpacking boxes and I've got a knife in my hand and I'm cutting a box and all of sudden I see myself cutting my wrist."

She takes her finger to her wrist and gasps, as if the blood were draining all over the floor. "Another time, it came at me and said, 'Your kids are grown. You don't need to be around anymore.'" The son of Jesus smiles, though she talks of blood and demons. "One woman at the clinic talked about slicing her wrist as if it were nothing at all."

She repeats: nothing at all.

"That's what I felt when I was thinking about cutting my wrist. I went *whoa*." She lets her wrist flop. "I could do it too," she whispers. "Like it was nothing."

For a long time we're quiet. The son of Jesus folds her body on a couch patterned with images of tropical birds.

The demons follow you after deliverance. That's what Ruth, the daughter of the son of Jesus, believes. Ruth has big red hair like steel wool. She thinks she's been followed for years. She was checked once after college for reinfestation. Nothing returned. The demon takes on a form and uses it to haunt you. Benjamin had a second look in November. The demons had returned. But Ruth believes it's only because he was delivered at age ten.

"Everyone's life goes to crap after deliverance," she says. "Sometimes the demons come back with a passion."

She had an old friend reinfested by religion. A Methodist girl who spent Saturdays at the club scene in Orlando preaching to girls with a loudspeaker while they threw up: Have you ever lied to any-one? Well then, you're a liar. Have you ever lusted for anyone? Well then, you're an adulterer. Have you ever thought hurtful things about a person? Well then, you're a murderer.

"I had six months. Most people have a year. God gives you a little grace time. The bottom line is now the enemy wants to destroy you. You're in the middle of the war and it's a continuous war."

Ruth went from a degree in Middle Eastern Studies at Florida State University to a job at Lowe's Hardware. She was also engaged to her longtime boyfriend. After deliverance, he left her. She burned all but one photograph of her ex-fiancé, which she occasionally looks at to remember how happy she'd once been. She tells herself: no—that's the past.

She believes she started seeing the casualties of war.

"You can't just pray one day and think it's over. If you go to war, if you don't have the cover, casualties come about. It's an active war. It can take months and years. You will see the casualties. I was a casualty. The bodies will stack up."

The moment a demonized person walks into the House of Women, Ruth starts praying. Ruth is tired of it—says it's exhausting. They had a woman stay with them a couple of months ago while she was receiving deliverance in Portal. The woman kept waking up in the night.

"The demon was there in front of her," Ruth says. "It had bright red eyes and it kept trying to choke her."

I ask why anyone would ever go through deliverance if life is always turning out to be so horrible.

"You could say you're safer, but then are you really doing what we're called on to do? What does it ever accomplish? You're safer if you sit in your house and do nothing. Won't you be starved for humanity?"

Ruth folds her socked feet under her legs.

"The scariest part," she says, "is that the world will always appear to be so much more perfect when you're demonized."

Marianne makes a bed for me atop the shag carpet of her floor. We take turns changing into our pajamas. "You go first," she says. It was too soon for nakedness.

"Are you ready?" she asks from the hallway. She must have changed in the bathroom because she enters wearing lavender pajama pants and a white top. The lights go off and her feet stick to the hardwood floors when she walks. Each part of her body adjusts itself, and the sound of her hair dropping on the pillow is like a light patter of rain.

"This is fun," Marianne says.

"Sure," I say.

"Just like a sleepover," she says. "I love sleepovers."

I don't respond.

"Do you like them?" she asks, her voice quieter this time, more careful.

"I do."

"Do you want to play Truth or Dare?"

"Maybe next time?" I say, gently as I can.

"Oh," she says. "Well, good night then."

"I'm sorry," I say, but the words are so quiet I doubt they reach her.

In the morning, the son of Jesus breaks egg yolks in a glass bowl. "You lose a lot of protein when you go into the spirit realm. It's exhausting. It requires a different kind of energy." Ruth's slicing a mango at a curved booth in the back of the kitchen. Marianne plays with her wet hair. "You'll be tired. A lot of times we'll sleep for a few days."

"Did you sleep well? Because I didn't," Marianne says. "I was talking to the Holy Spirit all night. I was seeing things. Getting salvation."

"Are you sure you don't want some fruit?" Ruth says, holding out a mango for me. "We have peaches, plums, bananas."

"We've been trying to eat really healthy," Marianne says. "Nothing processed."

Ruth nods. "I usually have almonds and yogurt for breakfast. But, of course, today's an exception. Today is deliverance. Today we can eat whatever we want."

"I wish they had a Trader Joe's here. I love Trader Joe's. Do you know about Trader Joe's? They should open one in Savannah. I bet it would do really well," Marianne says, glancing at the ceiling.

"Not me," Ruth says. "I hate Savannah. Too many demons."

"It's not as bad as Charleston," says Marianne. "You know, with repression."

The son of Jesus shovels two eggs and two sausages on my plate, and then points her spatula at me, the tip wet with oil. "Did you put on your armor today?"

"I don't know about any armor."

"Well, everyone has their own method," Marianne says. "I—"

"Armor!" the son of Jesus interrupts. She stands by the sink with the water rushing over a colander of plums and she starts shouting to God and moving her hands all over her body as if untying herself from a tangle of rope.

"Mom's fast at it," Ruth says.

"I usually put my armor on in the shower," Marianne says. "Sometimes I go to the shower and I say, 'Oh, God, I just don't feel like putting on my armor today.'" She holds a spoonful of eggs near her cheek.

"But you gotta do it," she says. "Why don't you do it now?" I stop chewing.

"Come on."

"Please, dear God, don't let the demons get me today," I say. "I don't know what I would do. I'm new." I lift my hands in the air and pretend to pour a bucket of water on my head.

"Amen!" The son of Jesus takes my plate. "Get changed, girls."

Marianne heads to her closet and throws a few items on the bed. "What do you think I should wear?" she asks. "I like looking nice for the Holy Spirit."

"Maybe the purple one?"

"Yeah," she says, drawing out her vowels. "You and Jesus both."

In Portal, when you look out past the fields that lay scattered and untilled you see patches of grass formed into the shape of fallen rags, trees dead so long the insides have been ingested by animals and used for better things, and the noon sun that filters through their cracked wood makes them glow in an unformed shape, no longer trees but lost things making their way across the land.

This afternoon, at deliverance, there's a woman crying in waves. Everyone has their eyes closed, searching for the enemy. There will be manifestations, women screaming. They'll find child abuse. Destroyers. Voices will churn in darkness. There will be victims of alcohol and victims of war. Tim will train new exorcists. He'll give them a thicker demon workbook. He'll tell them what to watch out for when the enemies attack. He will tell them to move around in the circle. He will take a particular liking to an apprentice who also sees a vision of a man trapped inside a tornado when trying to figure out what is wrong with a man whose wife ran away to Mexico. Daphne and Daisy will draw their thoughts on yellow legal pads. The drawings will be chaotic and dark: human bodies slashed apart.

I'm thinking about my physical reaction to their words—the way a bodily response feels like a verifiable symptom. The Greek language has many words to describe pain, but English does not. The word *pappapai* is physical pain whereas *otototoi* is a cry of grief.

Physical pain is corporeal and so wounds feel like evidence. We point to bloodied knees. We cough in napkins because yellowed phlegm means sick lungs. We stick lights down our throat to illuminate a gathering of strep. If the existence of pain is always, if possible, confirmed through the flesh, then the pain of the mind—psychic pain, tragic pain, the pain of broken hearts—must also desire such confirmation.

I think of the eight million soldiers who emerged shell-shocked from the trenches of World War I, when what we now call PTSD was called hysteria, and because hysteria was considered a female disease, unacceptable in males, soldiers expressed their trauma through the body. Snipers went blind. Soldiers who had bayoneted men in the face developed hysterical facial tics. Those who knifed men in the stomach were burdened with nauseating cramps. A soldier who was buried in the earth from a shell explosion later feared the dark.

Caleb worked six-month rotations as a contractor in Afghanistan and received three months' leave. Always gone, it seemed. Eden waited around the trailer. No work to do but twirl her wedding ring and sweat in the cool waters of the inflatable pool, wearing a cherry red swimsuit with wide coverage. Babies floated and splashed. She found items around the trailer to sell: turquoise jewelry, yellow crochets, porcelain figurines of ballerinas with their toes painted the most delicate pink. Caleb's promises weighed heavily in her gut. What did she want? Simple things. Home, children, security.

The minister got what he had hoped: Caleb quit his plans to save veterans. But contracting in Afghanistan, away from the trailer, and away from his youngest daughter, wasn't what the minister had in mind. Already he'd tired of seeing Eden checking her mail, wandering lonely around the trailer—doomed, even, to be a widow, he figured, with the way things were going. She hated the phases between deployments of relearning each other's habits and bodies.

One Saturday Caleb heard the minister's heavy footsteps coming up the hall. He was folding laundry, and the minister stepped inside and closed the door. "You need to be home for your wife," he said. The minister stood close and leaned forward. He set a thick finger on Caleb's chest.

"I'm going to count to three," Caleb said. "And I'm going to hurt you if you don't stop."

"One," he said. *Two.* Caleb remembered the time the minister walked into a car dealership and started praying and how they threw him out. He thought about the minister's sons-in-law and how they worshipped him. They couldn't even go out and buy a car without asking Tim to ask God. Caleb punched the minister. "I won't kneel to you," Caleb said. "Never." The minister wept on the ground with his eyes open, staring at a ceiling that never did rip open to show him heaven. He ran Caleb out of the house by chasing him into the yard with the immense gait of a bear. Caleb stuck around the trailer anyway. He and Eden fought, kissing and patting, and then separating with vicious talk, sitting quietly at mealtimes. Eden wasn't really on either side of things. A mind too long wound with Scripture sent her in circles between loyalty to her husband or to her father. The minister spoke to neither.

Weeks later, Caleb and Eden separated. Eden stayed at the trailer. Caleb drove off. Still, he wanted no one but Eden. All night he drove through sloping countryside, stopping at Mexican cafés, throwing back cervezas for the first time since the demon slipped out. He checked in at motels with coupon deals. In a week he was living on a boat at Lake Allatoona. He asked his son, Isaac, to think of a name for the boat. Together they decided on the name *Infidel.*

When the kids came to visit the *Infidel*, they dressed as pirates, and in the evening, when the water was dark and flat as a stain, Caleb dimmed the boat lights and kept the motor at a slow purr. Alligator fish, attracted to the noise, rose to the surface. Caleb and Isaac started shooting them. Blood everywhere.

In the summer, four months later, Caleb has a vision of me dying in a dark jungle mist. Hacking at creeper vines with a machete. Going in circles. There's no way out.

"I got my radar on you. Something is happening," he says.

Sometimes, if I wake, and a curtain twists in a night breeze, I think of him, and the others, slipping away in the dark.

One day he calls and suggests I rid my house of what he calls contaminated items: two bookcases, a table, and a bicycle. I ignore him. Months later, another bat comes into my room. Then a third time. When I listen to a recording of my exorcism, the power goes out. For these months, I wake at 1:46 in the morning. I'm fitting patterns together that aren't really there, the same way Caleb might have done, stringing a narrative through his past that made sense in light of the war's atrocity. But it's not the specificity of Caleb's demons that I believe, only that there's something happening to my psychology. I wait two days and then I do it. I push each item onto the street. A neighbor takes the bicycle and stores it in his yard. Every day when I look out the window I can see the bicycle and I'm reminded of illness.

I had a friend who used to believe in a theology of angels and demons. One night he woke up and the barn across the street was burning. Three black figures ran from it. The neighbors burned the barn to rid it of demons. He was afraid of the dark. The local minister told him to look into the darkness and say: *tell me your name.* When he left his Pentecostal upbringing behind, he also left those beliefs.

"The point is," he said, "that we're just slipping from one hallucination to another."

I'm thinking of this story because I'm watching a clip of three soldiers urinating on the corpses of Taliban fighters. The media keeps asking how this atrocity could happen. I no longer find myself asking that question. I've come to understand how easily, how intrusively, a heightened situation can make us, any of us, slip.

The unknown can come for us. And when it does, it's devastating. For America, the unknown came on 9/11. The mythic bridge building gone. The moment that shined a light on everything that preceded it.

I drive four hours from Iowa City to Missouri to see him. He won't stop telling me it's an emergency that he needs to talk. The image of bat pushes me back to him. Caleb is damp from the rains. There are white flakes on his cheekbones from a recent sunburn. His eyes are dark and worried as if someone reached inside and scooped out all the blue.

His mother lives in Columbia, a half hour from Centralia, and when I ask Caleb whether his mother and stepfather know that he sees demons, he shakes his head. He doesn't care. "They'll figure it out." His stepfather is sitting on a rocking chair, watching football. The stepdad is eager to tell me about the moment he heard about the chopper crash in Afghanistan. "Caleb called from Savannah," he says. "He wanted to let us know that he was still alive."

We drive toward St. Louis. Caleb hangs his arm out the car window. The air stings with diesel fumes. His kids are in the backseat, the two from his ex-wife, Isaac and Isabel. They sit close.

"I thought you believed God brought you and Eden together?"

"We make choices in our life," he says. "I was wrong before about God. I still had learning to do. I was putting everything God gave me into what I thought I wanted. Not what it will be."

"There was a man who came for deliverance," I say. "But they couldn't save him. I saw him hiding out at some motel wearing camo."

"Luciferian," he says. "You know I wouldn't be surprised if Tim were a Luciferian. I don't think he's ever been through deliverance."

"It says in his book he has." Caleb doesn't answer. "You didn't read the book, did you?"

"That crap?" He shakes his head.

"You told me to read it."

"Things were different then."

"You don't believe anymore?"

Caleb slits his eyes and rolls his head toward me. "I've been through too much. I see it every day. It's real." He stuffs Copenhagen under his lip and mumbles through it. "Don't get me wrong," he says. "They saved me. They do good things, amazing things, but they're fucking *crazy*. They messed up my friends Mary and Chris so bad. You meet Mary and Chris? They infected Mary's mind, made her think she was a terrible person—they get in your head." He points at his head and looks at me. "Chris couldn't even deploy—he had to miss work to take care of her."

In St. Louis, the Arch rushes like a geyser across the sky. Its metal twists sunlight. We stop so Isaac and Isabel can take a ride in a tourist helicopter that flies at its height. Isaac mourns for a bird killed in the chopper blades.

In 1973, forty-eight years of military records, from 1912 to 1960, burned in a fire at the National Personnel Records Center in St. Louis, echoing a similar event that happened in September 1940, when the War Office repository in London burned in the Blitz. Sixty percent of British military records from World War I were gone. The events have taken on new meaning ever since trauma scholar Judith Herman wrote about how our ordinary response to atrocity is to banish it from consciousness.

We drive out of the city at dusk, through stretches of dead fields, places where the corn is green and quiet as cocoons. Everywhere hay bales glow solid and white.

In Centralia, Caleb slumps in his seat. He spreads his hands apart as if introducing me. "This is where I would've ended up. Working on a corn farm. Maybe in jail. Steve's in jail. Roy's in jail. Sandra's a coke addict." Old friends. "It blew her mind I had a job."

He asks if I know about last roll-call ceremony. It's the ceremony where the commanders call the names of the soldiers one final time. They play "Taps," or "Butterfield's Lullaby." "Saddest song I've ever heard," he says.

The sun looks like someone took a fork to it and rubbed it all over the horizon. Clouds, orange with its light, gather like fumes on the edges of trees.

"Kip Jacoby," Caleb calls out. "Kip A. Jacoby," he says. "Sergeant Kip A. Jacoby."

We wait.

"See," he says. "No response."

Caleb thinks he saw his dead friends the other day, all of them standing in a line on a grassy hill. And he describes them right there with his eyes closed, his hands moving in loops ahead of him, as if he were drawing them out of the sky. They were wearing their flight suits.

"What does it mean?" I say.

"It means they were all home," he says. "They were finally home. I asked Kip if he could talk. I said, 'Please, buddy.' But Kip said no. 'Well, why not, Kip?' And Kip said, 'It's different over here.'"

I imagine the first time Caleb put on his uniform, getting it caught in the wind, making him look falsely full and big, a kite ready to sail.

• • •

After his children are tucked into bed, we take his mother's car, a Lexus with leather seats softened with a weekly oil. He gives me a distant look. "Are you tired?" I ask. He laughs. "I haven't slept in a long, long time." We're like teenagers or thieves. We drive into the dusk. Caleb starts talking about post-Vietnam Harley gangs. "Loyal to their gangs," he says. "What now?" He says that after war, soldiers still have to find ways to vent their soldierness. "Contracting is one of those things. Sixty-day rotations, home thirty days. That's what I'm doing. Venting my soldierness." He changes the topic. "The spoils of war," he says. "Have to give spoils to guys. If you don't you're not going to have guys to fight the war. Back to the Greeks and the Romans, to now. Always gave away land or something."

"What does America give you?"

"America gives you pain-killers."

We're somewhere outside Columbia, a suburban area where the restaurants are bright at closing time. Caleb pulls over on a steep side street. It's crossed by railroad tracks and disappears into the woods. We find a dim café to order drinks. It's already dark. We sit down and the air-conditioning dries my eyes.

Caleb pulls a plastic bag of tobacco out of his pocket and gathers enough for his cheeks. "I told you not to go see April," he says. He taps the table. "What's been going on?" His eyes wander in the spaces around me. He leans forward and whispers, "Did I tell you what I saw?"

"You didn't tell me anything."

"Did I tell you about the big old bat that's been following you around?"

"So I told you about the bat?"

He pets his chin. He shakes a finger at me like I'm playing a joke on him. "I told you about the bat?"

I didn't tell him about the bat. I pour salt on the table. I press my thumb into it. "Did I tell you about the bat?"

"You didn't tell me about the bat?" he says.

I take out my notebook and draw a picture of the bat in my dreams. "Okay, it's your turn," I say. He makes a waving motion with his hands. He doesn't want to look. "Freaks me out," he says.

A group of truckers walk by and crowd a booth across from us. Caleb lowers his voice so they can't hear. "What I saw," he says, "is this big old bat wrapping its wings around you. Its nails were long, rawhide, and dirty."

I mention the real bat and the rabies shots.

"*That fucker,*" he says in a low hush. "You know, I've heard of this—" He pauses. "This *bat man*. He fucked with my buddy once. It flew over his truck. Wing span big as a plane." Caleb gathers his hands beneath his chin. "Well," he says, "it hasn't attached."

For a while we don't speak. We stare into light streaming through dirty windows.

"This is just the way life works after deliverance: horrible, scary thing. Life pans out. Another horrible, scary thing. Life pans out. For a few weeks following deliverance I was a failure at everything. I failed at this and this and this. But it was just a test. After I got through that, it just went away. It didn't come back. But I honestly believe the demons come back sevenfold."

I tell him the son of Jesus thought it was the suicide demon.

"She doesn't know shit. She thinks everything is suicide. Every time we do deliverance everybody has suicide. She's always knee-deep in suicide." He scratches his skin, yellow like wax in the street-light; like maybe it could come off and get stuck under his nails. "When the Destroyer came after me," he adds, "it was probably the scariest thing I've ever seen."

The waitress says they're closing. A janitor sweeps the floor with her eyes closed. We take our drinks outside to a small iron table chained to other tables overlooking an alley. Yellow umbrellas bloom from their centers. The streetlights leave only a small circle of black above us, faint with stars.

"It was hard for you to come here, wasn't it. I know."

"Why do you think that?"

"There's something," he said. "Following you." He pointed at the space behind me. "I saw it on you when you arrived. It's from talking to Brian's sister April. It transferred. I've been trying to get through to you. I check up on you every month or so."

The janitor stops to look at us through the window.

"You still don't know why you met me, do you."

"Did you know they used to shoot people with PTSD?" I say. "These young guys in the trenches."

"You don't know what you've gotten yourself into."

He starts speaking in metaphors without context. I don't know what he's saying. "There's a broke-down train," he says. "Okay, now get it from point A to point B."

"I don't know," I keep saying. "I don't know."

"You still don't know why you met me, do you." He shakes his head. "Tell me what you thought of me when we met. You think I was a dumb, crazy guy? Is that what you thought? You can tell me. Tell me everything. I'll tell you whatever you want to know. First tell me, why did you meet me?"

"Are you worried?"

"Simple question."

He says it as if he wants to take all of me, arrange it on a table, and look at my organs in harsh light.

"I knew you were demonically tormented," he repeats. "You laughed when I told you about the demons. I knew your generational curse line was very strong. Some occult shit in there. Oh, and I don't know, I can't explain it. I guess I figured you were a man-hater or something. It seemed like you never even wanted to talk

207

to me. I felt bad for you. I felt very bad, in fact, because I knew it would take you a long time to learn what this all meant."

He sucked his straw black with Coke. "I've told you the intimate details of my life. The things I'd never tell anyone else. You never tell me anything about your life."

I'm drawing shapes in my notebook and trying not to look at him.

"What do you want to know?" I ask.

He's silent and hunched with his head up like a turtle. "Have you figured out your objective?" he says. "Have you figured out why you met me?"

"There are demons," I say, hoping that's the answer he wants.

"That's a little obvious by now."

He drags his fingers from his cheekbones to his chin the way someone might remove a mask.

"You don't understand any of this," he says. "You don't know what you've gotten yourself into. You went and saw that gal. I warned you. I said this thing is going to come after you. You're kinda fucked right now, but I can help you."

I'm writing down what he says in my notebook until it's darkened by the shadow of his hand. He pulls my pen from my fingers. He closes my notebook. He takes it. He hides it in his lap. "This has nothing to do with the goddamned book," he says.

The headlights of a passing car catch Caleb's face, and his eyes stay wide and motionless in its glare. He waits until it passes. "I'm frustrated with your rational background. You ask too many questions. You see everything too logically. This is freaking spiritual warfare."

He spreads his legs and sinks between them.

"You're my subject." This word quiets him.

"What?" He leans back, deflated, as if someone took a pin to him and some air seeped out.

"Give me my pen."

"You've never trusted me. You've never trusted Caleb. All this time and you've never trusted Caleb."

"I got in your truck. I drove with you to a trailer in Portal."

He shakes his head. "I want you to figure out why you met me."

I tell him he clearly has an answer to this question and that he should just tell me.

"Will you let me pray," he says.

"Why?"

"I can help you," he says. "Take my hand."

I flex my hand into a ball and set it in his open palm. Then I pull it away. "I don't want to." His eyeballs move beneath closed lids like things turning over in the womb.

He stands up, heads into the street, and starts jogging. He stops before the railroad tracks beneath a streetlight. In the solitary yellow glow, he raises his arms. He could be a demon now himself.

"What?" I shout.

"Nothing," he says. He jogs back. "Just wait."

A long stream of prayers comes from his mouth. The streets are wide and sleek and black like rivers. A moaning rises from the distance. The wind is coming, coming down from across the agricultural fields sour with the smells of opossum and corn rot.

"What's happening?" I say.

I have the sensation that we're lying down, or that the world is moving and we're standing still. Bits of trash scrape the asphalt and gather by the tracks. A gathering of cups and soda cans swirls and rises like a tower.

One by one the streetlights darken.

I lean toward the dark.

"Power outage?"

"They're here." He drums his hands on the table.

"Who?"

"The whole fucking army is here." He reaches his arms above his head and opens them like a ballerina.

"What does that mean?"

He describes something from a war movie I've never seen, a movie where horses die and men are blown apart in trenches and the air is full of screaming.

A figure darts between bushes across the street.

"Wait," he says. He recognizes my stare. He recognizes it as his own. "You see them, don't you? That's what I asked," he says. "That's what I prayed. I want you to see them. Just a little."

"It's just a person," I say.

"I can see you in the spirit realm," he says. "I can see you right now. It's amazing. You know who you are? You're fucking Joan of Arc." He talks like a general who's already imagined the slaughter and the victory.

"You need to hold my hand," he says. "The only way to defeat this army is to do it together. You can't do this alone. I can't either."

His hand is there, calling to me, dark from the sun in Afghanistan.

"I don't want to hold your hand."

"They will hurt you if you let them. You're letting them hurt you. Don't let them hurt you. Please, hold my hand." He breathes with the delicate throbbing stress of a small animal. "Join me," he says. "Please, join my army."

He quiets to let his words settle and arrange themselves. A moth flickers by his head like a small, loose flame.

"You think Afghanistan is scary? You think a fucking IED is scary? Rockets? Dead guys everywhere? It's nothing compared to this war. This war is much, *much* worse." His fingers wave me in. "Take my hand. There's no good way out. Take my hand," he says. "Join my army."

I try to imagine what he sees: the army dying in waves on flat, burning fields.

"I know what you've been going through with the enemy," he says. "You're the skinny guy with an AK-47 and you're getting pummeled by a huge army. You're getting shot in the face. You're wounded. There's fire all around you. You're on the ground, limping. Don't you think it would be better to gather an army? Resupply. Move under the cover of darkness?"

Now he's pacing back and forth, gesticulating like a deposed king in a tragic play.

"We both have weapons. If we put them together, we'll at least have a chance against the enemy. You're taking some serious fire. I'd love to put up some cover for you. I'll cover your back if you cover mine."

Finally I take his hand and he quiets. He whispers to God in the dark. An oily twist of hair on his forehead curls like a hook. He releases. "Now," he says. "I have to pee."

We stand to leave. As we approach the car his hand flutters in front of mine. "Give me your cup." I set it in his hand and he throws it in a garbage can's open mouth.

"See," he says. "I'm a gentleman."

Caleb is staying with his mother and I'm staying at a hotel. He'll drop me off. "Father," he says, "show us the hotels."

Father shows us dead ends, neighborhoods thick with two-story homes, and the parking lot at Taco Bell. I nod off, forehead smashed to the window. He flicks my shoulder and I jerk awake in the parking lot of a Best Western.

Blue pool light shimmers up the hotel walls. There's the faint sound of a late-night swimmer. The murmur of television from an open window. The asphalt sparkles around us, same as the sky.

He asks if I'm afraid. I say I don't really know. He investigates shadows between cars. He insists on walking to the desk with me. He says it's following me.

"What brings you to Missouri?" the receptionist asks. Caleb stands spiderlike by the brochure rack. It's an absurd question at the moment. My troubled laugh begins. First as a shiver. Then it spreads to Caleb. The receptionist watches. "Missouri" is all I manage to say, laughing. "Missouri." The credit card hovers in midswipe. "All right," she says. "You don't have to tell."

I say good night to Caleb. He slips back into the Lexus, merges into traffic on Interstate 70.

Rooms leak the sounds of television, people chatting, beds creaking. A long arm of light drapes over the bed in my room. I bolt the door and stand near the television. I turn all the lights on and the shadows deepen. I know I won't be able to sleep. Caleb's words are churning. I'm looking behind me, under the bed, in the closet. I stay in the bathroom. Red veins bloom in my eyes like coral growths. I run the water. My mouth foams with toothpaste.

I'm annoyed with Caleb, and I write him a message to let him know. I tell him that now I feel like I'm being followed. I want him to know my fear, to see what he's done. My phone rings. It vibrates diagonally across the carpet like a mouse. It's him. I pick it up and before I can say hello, he says, "Is it human or beast?"

"You don't need to call," I tell him.

"I'm coming," he says.

"Please, don't. Aren't you tired?"

"I'm coming," he says.

I step out of the bathroom and look at the door. I still have the phone pressed to my ear. I hear the sound of a car engine. The sound of tires. "It's too late," he says. "I've already turned around." He stays on the line, noting passing objects: ramp, exit, parking lot, entrance, floor, door, door, door. Then, *I'm here.*

The eyehole darkens.

I let him in. The metal bolt catches quick as a bite. I release it. He steps inside swinging his lowered head to the left and to the right, like a bull releasing himself from unwanted reins. "Where is it?"

I point at the clock. It's one forty-six in the morning.

"Fancy that," he says, and he takes a bow at the clock's hard truth.

"You planned that."

"No way."

Caleb strides across the carpet. "What's the first thing you do when the enemy enters? You make yourself at home. Take your shoes off. Stay a while."

The room has two beds. He sits on one and I on the other. He twirls a loose string on the comforter. A long mirror hangs on the wall between us.

"I'm here. There's nothing to be afraid of." His grin twists like smoke. Take your jacket off. Lean back. Relax."

Suddenly he leaps into the air and falls vertically onto the bed, landing with a gentle, fluttering bounce. He poses the way a woman might in want of portrait: elbow bent, palm flat to hoist a heavy, smiling head. Legs are stacked and curved. Toes, pointed.

"What was your most recent nightmare?" he asks.

"A bat. But wingless."

"Good," he says. "It's lost power."

I laugh and he follows. "Okay, you have authority over this thing. You can make it go away.

"Say, 'Father.'"

"Father."

"Say, 'I command all things unclean or foul.'"

"I command all things unclean or foul."

"Say, 'to leave.'"

"To leave."

"Say, 'in the name of Jesus Christ of Nazareth.'"

"In the name of Jesus Christ of Nazareth."

"'Son of the Living God.'"

"Son of the Living God."

I start scratching my neck where the bat touched me in my dream.

"Interesting," he says, and he jumps to the floor. "You know how to make a dog obedient? You get it on the floor, press your hand against its neck." Caleb is on the floor demonstrating dog submission, pressing one palm flat on the ground. "That's what the Destroyer was doing." Lamplight thickens on his forehead. "Let me pray," he says.

He wraps his hand around my neck, and his fingers curl like a collar over my throat. It's time for the killing. But instead he presses the top of my head into his hands, and I just sort of hang there, suspended, like something growing out of him. An act of saving. I wait, playing dead, while he speaks to God.

"Ah, it's in your ear," he says, and I fall back like those people on television struck by faith.

Now he's in the desk chair, tilted back, feet on the bed.

He shoots me a relaxed look like he wants to smoke a cigar, watch football, shoot the shit. Then he pushes his foot against the TV and sends his chair into a quiet spin.

"You've been dating someone, haven't you?"

I tell him I have.

"You know what I think? I think he was a conduit for evil. The demon worked through him. It's the whole sex before marriage thing. Now you and him are soul ties. They're hard to break. Took me forever to break my soul tie with Krissy." He wipes his nose with the back of his hand. "That's how the demon got power over you."

He mulls over knitted fingers.

"But if you think about it, it's almost funny. It's just a stupid little bat."

"Just a stupid little bat," I say.

214

A plane comes into view and blinks on its diagonal journey to the ground.

A rough laugh overtakes him, and then quiets to something faint and grave. Neither of us is sure anymore what's funny and what isn't.

"Let me show you what the bat did to you." And he stands up and comes toward me and uses his arms like wings to pump himself across the room. I keep my limbs close to my body. "Turn around," he says. And he does what the bat did. He wraps. My head gets pressed sideways into his chest, making it hard to breathe, and I just sort of stay there, stiff in his arms. "I'm not going to let go," he says. "Join my army." I feel his breath beating into a single spot on my cheek. "Is this what it was like when the bat came?" Caleb holds me there, humming and rocking, pretending and believing. "This bat," he says. "He had bundled you up. He was swaying and holding you. He had you all wrapped up tight in his wings. And you know what else? He was singing to you. The bat sang to you. A really sad song. He was singing you a lullaby. It was the most beautiful song in the world. Are you listening to this lullaby? I wonder."

When the Sirens sang to Odysseus they sang about the truth of how the men suffered at the war in Troy.

"I won't let you go," he says. "I won't let you go."

I wiggle away. I'm watching him now like the enemy.

"It's the saddest song in the world. Listen." He leans into me and I have to push against him to support his weight. And there it is, his heart, *beating, beating, beating*—like a song.

He crawls like an insect onto the bed. He looks at me.

Lul-la-by, he says, *lul-la-by.*

"It's the saddest song in the world. Listen."

Kip Jacoby. Sergeant Kip Jacoby. Sergeant Kip A. Jacoby. He lets the words hang in the quiet. He makes me feel the death.

Lullaby. The song that bridges waking and sleep.

A POSTSCRIPT FOR
THE IRRITABLE HEART

In March 1969 a Vietnam veteran walked into the Boston VA outpatient clinic and told the psychiatrist on duty that he was convinced his buddies were trying to kill him. He was part of Charlie Company, 1st Battalion, and his platoon was under orders to enter the village of My Lai in Northern Vietnam with their guns firing. The village, their commander said, was full of Vietcong. But when the soldiers arrived and the initial smoke cleared, they found elderly men, women, and babies whom they raped, tortured, and executed. Survivors lived by hiding beneath corpses. The veteran didn't shoot. He threw his gun to the side and watched. The other soldiers knew this about him, and when the killings were over, the soldiers in his platoon turned to him and said that if he ever uttered a word about what happened in My Lai, they'd kill him too. One of the soldiers said they might kill him anyway just in case.

The veteran told the story to social worker Sarah Haley, and it was her first day on the job. Haley accepted the veteran's story at face value. She had no illusions about war. The fact that war is sometimes women getting gang-raped, their bodies mutilated, infants shot point-blank in their mother's arms, bodies moaning in piles. Her father was an assassin with the Office of Strategic Services in North Africa during World War II. She grew up on such stories.

But when the rest of the VA staff met to discuss the case, they had already determined a diagnosis. They said the veteran was a paranoid schizophrenic. In other words, they didn't believe him. No one knew about My Lai—the newspaper reports weren't out.

"Most American psychiatrists," said Arthur Blank, a psychiatrist who worked with Sarah Haley at the Boston clinic, "based their encounters with Vietnam veterans on the official view that no such thing as PTSD existed."

Judith Herman, author of *Trauma and Recovery*, writes that people who have survived atrocities often tell their stories in a "highly emotional, contradictory, and fragmented manner that undermines their credibility and thereby serves the twin imperatives of truth-telling and secrecy." Recognizing the truth leads to recovery, but if secrecy prevails, then the story of the traumatic event won't exist as a verbal narrative, she argues, but as a symptom. It's Herman's theory that despite a great deal of literature on the subject, there's still an ongoing debate about whether PTSD is a real phenomenon. Because to study trauma, Herman says, is to encounter the human capacity for evil.

It's no wonder that PTSD has had more than eighty different names in the last hundred years: neurasthenia, hysteria, war hysteria, irritable heart, soldier's heart, disorderly conduct of the heart, combat exhaustion, combat fatigue, neurocirculatory asthenia, shell shock, war neurosis, fright neurosis, trauma neurosis, combat stress reaction, stress response syndrome, acute stress disorder, concentration camp syndrome, Vietnam syndrome, war sailor syndrome. French physicians of the Napoleonic Wars simply called it *nostalgia*.

It's a condition constantly refusing definition. It's as if the illness itself were enacting its own symptoms.

When the *DSM-II* was published in 1968, there was no specific listing for the trauma produced by war. So in 1969, when American troop involvement escalated in Vietnam, there was still no term available to psychiatrists. They were required to use the language of civilian disease.

Historically hysteria was considered a distinctly female problem. Elaine Showalter writes in *The Female Malady* about such gender expectations of soldiers during World War I: "When all signs of physical fear were judged as weakness and where alternative to combat—pacifism, conscientious objection, desertion, even suicide—were viewed as unmanly, men were silenced and immobilized and forced, like women, to express their conflicts through the body."

Hippocrates might be to blame, insisting that an errant womb triggered madness—a womb loose in the body, floating ghostlike among other organs, disrupting nerves, seeking the brain. In the dialogues of Timaeus, Plato wrote that the womb delighted in sweet smells but fled from fetid smells, ordaining the womb with the qualities of a conscious being, an "animal within an animal." In early Christianity, evil spirits were thought to ascend from beneath the female, move up her genitals and reside in her womb, filling her with madness. Male soldiers, wombless, had no such concern.

But eight thousand men emerged from the trenches of World War I suffering hysteric symptoms. Doctors used the term *shell shock* and maintained that hysterical symptoms of men were not psychological in origin but a result of physical damage to the brain and central nervous system. Military doctors believed the physical impact of an exploding shell caused damage to the brain and nervous system. No one wanted to imagine a world in which male soldiers were vulnerable to hysteria. Finally it became clear that many hysteric soldiers had never been in the proximity of a shell explosion. These soldiers were considered moral invalids. Military doctors then decided on two categories: *shell shock commotion* and *shell shock emotion*. Those who suffered from shell shock emotion received no honors or care.

The denial continued. In fact, the history of PTSD could easily be characterized by this word—our denial, specifically, of the reality of war and its effect on the human psyche. In 1944 Army Chief of Staff General George C. Marshall blamed what we now call PTSD on America's educational system. Army psychiatrist William Menninger blamed PTSD on American society, which was at "the immature stage of development, characterized by, 'I want what I want when I want it, and the hell with the rest of the world.'" Philip Wylie, in his 1942 book *Generation of Vipers,* blamed PTSD on "moms." He called PTSD *momism,* or "the problem of domineering mothers nurturing weak and immature sons." At the back of the book, Wylie included a quiz: "Are You a Mom?"

War, Showalter believes, is the only time in history when men have occupied a central position in the history of madness.

ACKNOWLEDGMENTS

This book features men and women who have been through traumatic experiences. I am grateful to these individuals for sharing their stories. I've changed certain names and biographical details.

I'd like to thank the National Endowment for the Arts for giving me the time and financial means to write this book. Thank you also to the Iowa Arts Council and the Truman Capote Literary Trust. Thank you to all the wonderful people at Scribner who believed in this book. My deepest thanks to my brilliant, tireless editor, Paul Whitlatch, who made this book better for his insight and talent. Thank you, Alexis Gargagliano, for your warmth and exuberance and for believing in this book from the beginning. My amazing agent, PJ Mark, and his team at Janklow & Nesbit.

I'm so grateful to have had the support of so many friends. Thank you especially to Zaina Arafat, Dini Parayitam, Tom Quach, Van Choojitarom, Nina Feng, Benjamin Shattuck, Daniel Cesca, David Busis, Joseph Tiefenthaler, Liz Weiss, Emilie Trice, Mike Scalise, Ossian Foley, Micah Stack, Dylan Nice, Rachel Yoder, Amy Butcher, Danny Khalastchi, Tommy Wisdom, Kristen Radtke, Benjamin Nugent, Leslie Jamison, Jennifer Kim, Anita Wickramasinghe, Casey Walker, Karen Thompson Walker, Ngwah-Mbo Nana Nkweti, Sidhartha Rao, Tim Denevi, Cutter Wood, and Andre Perry. And thank you to Mallika Rao for being one of the first to encourage me to write. I'd like to thank Benjamin Busch, Doug Stanton, and David Morris for help with fact-checking.

Thank you to my incredible teachers throughout the years: David Bain, Susan Lohafer, Bonnie Sunstein, Patricia Foster, John D'Agata, Robin Hemley, Michelle Hunevan, David Hamilton, Andrew Sean Greer, Ethan Canin, Samantha Chang. Thank you to Connie Brothers, Deb West, and Jan Zenisek.

Thank you to Dina Nayari for your encouragement during hard times. One day I will get ice cream with you. Thank you to my reader Kerry Howley, who is brilliant beyond words and can take a razor blade to a manuscript like no one else. Most of all, I'm indebted to my friend and reader Kyle Minor not only for his wisdom and contagious love of the written word but because he made it possible to go on when it no longer seemed possible.

Thank you to the best brother I could ever ask for, Benjamin Percy, whose love and support sustain me. And to my amazing sister-in-law, Lisa. I'm so grateful for your wisdom and strength. And to my parents, who have never once doubted a single dream of mine.

While researching this book, I consulted the following works: *In the Devil's Snare* by Mary Beth Norton; *Lone Survivor* by Marcus Luttrell; *Trauma and Recovery* by Judith Herman; *The Female Malady* by Elaine Showalter; "PTSD in *DSM-III*: A Case in the Politics of Diagnosis and Disease" by C. J. Wilbur; *Unclaimed Experience: Trauma, Narrative, and History* by Cathy Caruth; *Beyond the Pleasure Principle* by Sigmund Freud; *The Origin of Consciousness in the Bicameral Mind* by Julian Jayne; *Victory Point* by Ed Darack; *Odysseus in America: Combat Trauma and the Trials of Homecoming* and *Achilles in Vietnam* by Jonathan Shay; *On Killing* by Lt. Col. Dave Grossman; "Memories of Iraq haunted soldier until suicide" by Halimah Abdullah, *McClatchy Report*, May 25, 2008; "Healing for Peace: Traditional Healers and Post-War Reconstruction in Southern Mozambique" by Alcinda Manuel, *Journal of Peace Psychology*, 1997; *Spirit Possession and Exorcism: History, Psychology, and Neurobiology* by Patrick McNamara, Ph.D.

Thank you to Captain Brady, who shared with me his story of Operation Red Wings. I'm grateful to everyone who gave hours of their time to be interviewed for this book.

Jen Percy, a graduate of the Iowa Writers' Workshop, has received a Truman Capote Fellowship, an Iowa Arts Fellowship, the Pushcart Prize, and a National Endowment for the Arts grant. Her essays have appeared or are forthcoming in *Harper's*, *The New Republic*, *The New York Times Magazine*, *Esquire*, and elsewhere.